CW00520944

PRAISE FOR *WEBSITE MASTI*
OWNERS WHO DON'T ᴊᴘᴇᴀᴋ ᴛᴇᴄʜ

"The front door of your business is your website. Fiona's book will guide you to create a welcoming and engaging website that will have the best prospects asking - scratch that - begging to be invited in."

Mike Michalowicz
author of Get Different and Profit First

PRAISE FOR THE WEBSITE MASTERY METHOD:

"I want to congratulate you on this process for refreshing a website. This has helped me enormously and I also believe most importantly that the quality and technical knowledge you have is extremely credible. Thank you!"
Proprietor, Corporate Coaching Sector

"From the beginning of the process, you made it as easy as possible, keeping the technological speak to a minimum so that I completely understood what was happening with the new site and what was required from me at every stage."
Managing Director, Estate Agency Sector

"This gave us a strong foundation for the rest of the development process, and the end result is a website that is visually striking and perfectly projects our brand."
Managing Director, Customer Service Sector

"We are really pleased with our new site - produced with little fuss, on time and on budget - PLUS we are seeing a great increase in traffic, the whole purpose of the exercise."
Managing Director, Technology Sector

"You produced a very professional and easy to understand website for our charity about a very complicated medical condition. It was a huge relief to someone as IT illiterate as me."
Chairperson, Charity Sector

"You listened to my ideas, gave us time to discuss them and made great suggestions on how to improve them, but most of all I valued your business advice and wisdom. It really changed my view on how I should move forward."
Proprietor, Ecommerce Sector

"The website looked great and we were proud to launch it – six months later we realised we had seen an increase of £126,000 in online sales – now we think you're a bloody bargain!"
Marketing Manager, Manufacturing Sector

WEBSITE
M A S T E R Y

FOR BUSINESS OWNERS
WHO DON'T SPEAK TECH

The Non-Coder's Guide to Launching a High-Performing
Website that Boosts Your Traffic, Conversion Rates
and Business Growth

FIONA ALLMAN-TREEN

Dedicated to every business owner with a dream.

Whatever it is you do, nobody does it like you.

CONTENTS

FOREWORD

BY CHRIS CHITTY
THE ULTIMATE CONFIDENCE COACH

I am so grateful to be asked to write the foreword to this extraordinary book...

Fiona is a fabulous friend who I met a few years ago when coaching her on maintaining momentum in her business, and so I am privileged to know her humour, her vast knowledge and also her desire to not only run a successful business, but to use the vehicle of that business to create a better, more effective and ethical business world.

I invite you to read this book like you are having a paid consultation with one of the world's leading website experts... because you are...

Read it as though you paid thousands for the knowledge contained within... read it with that intensity... and expect to find diamonds of inspiration, ideas and creation that not only relate to your website... but potentially your whole organisation.

If your website is "gathering dust", just another item on your to do list, or a mystery to you as you just hate tech - then this book is for you!

Why?

Well, it doesn't feel like a technical book, although there is plenty of technical detail. It's written in a way to inspire you, and excite you about the vast possibilities and opportunities of your site... and as you will see as the pages unfold, there are so many opportunities.

Fiona owns her subject... She has over 2 decades of experience and hundreds of client success stories... some of which are detailed within.

She writes as she talks... with enthusiasm, energy and a deep love for your business and your success... that's who she is at her core!

This book is like having your own website expert to hand 24/7.

Enjoy!

HOW TO KNOW IF THIS BOOK IS FOR YOU

You are the Owner / Manager of an established six or seven-figure business with plans to grow rapidly over the next 5 years, but you're stuck with a website that does nothing for you and you don't know what it *could* be doing to make your vision a reality. You're already successful – look how far you've already come in your industry and that great reputation you're building every day! You know it could be more though, serve more people in more places, do more of the sort of work you love to do – but doing more of the same isn't cutting it anymore and you know, deep down, that what got you this far won't get you where you want to go *next*.

To make it happen you need more than just more traffic to your site, you need the right <u>kind</u> of visitors, people who need and value what you offer – in a website which appeals to them and they form a connection with as soon as they see it. Then there are all those repetitive tasks that eat up your day or your team's time – sending out brochures, following up enquiries, calculating quotes, or maybe just delivering that customer experience – how will you manage all that if the enquiries suddenly DID hit the roof?

You've tried sorting this out yourself (or with a member of your team), redesigning your website over and over again – perhaps you've even invested in expensive online advertising to get those numbers up – but nothing's changing and, frankly, speaking with some web developers and creators is not helping. It's like they're speaking another language...

What you need most right now is someone who gets what you're trying to achieve, really gets it. Who knows and understands your target audience and what *they* need to see and experience on your site to really engage with you and your Company AND has all the technical know-how to build in features which take work off your desk, add value to your visitors and showcase how great you really are at what you do. This transforms them from visitors into customers and raving fans, so you see greater results and your business becomes everything you wanted it to be.

This is what my team and I do - and have done every day for over two decades – and this book gives you a step-by-step guide on WHAT you need to include to grow your business online and WHY it matters, without having to learn HOW to code it yourself.

I've walked every kind of Business Owner, Charity Founder and Public Sector Consultant through this process, creating websites for every imaginable industry (yes, even *those* ones...!), delivering enormously successful sites promoting individual brands, generating income for good causes, delivering online training and coaching to literally millions of people across the world and sold record numbers of products of every kind - from pants to paintings!

This book walks you through our unique, *proven*, tried and tested five-step process of launching a successful website for your business – one that acts as a marketing <u>machine</u>; attracting, engaging and converting right-fit clients to your product or service. Every. Single. Day. I've included insights I've also shared on our You Tube channel (www.youtube.com/@fatpromotions), articles and blogs over the years – now expanded into a single, sequential system for you to follow and apply to your own individual business or organisation.

I'll share authentic case study examples from our own commercial experience, demonstrating how applying this strategy in their business has delivered fantastic results for business owners just like you time and time again. PLUS, to keep you on track, throughout the book you'll find Checkpoints: pages where you can check in with yourself, answer some basic questions and feel certain that you're taking in the key points which will serve you best in reaching your business vision. To help you in this, at the end of the book you will find links to many of the resources and tools I mention, including our free Online Strategy Assessment so you can see what's blocking your website success, and what you can do about it.

So why am I publicly sharing all of this information, over two decades of experience and expertise invested in delivering award-winning websites for business, charities and public sector projects - including how my team and I do what we do – isn't that *crazy*??

I don't think so – and I'll tell you why. Because every business owner, entrepreneur and ambitious, mission-driven human being I've ever met has told me *exactly* the same thing:

I CAN TELL YOU WHAT TO DO, BUT NOBODY DOES IT LIKE I DO

HOW DO I KNOW THIS WORKS?

I still recall the first time I saw the internet. I had worked in graphic design for a few years creating brochures and marketing materials for various businesses when a friend showed me this "amazing new thing" he had found - which turned out to be a web page for a rock band. A bunch of us clustered around his computer to watch a single page load (incredibly slowly, this was the days of dial-up internet connections!) and then - the truly amazing part - a photo which moved when you hovered over it with the mouse! This all sounds as exciting as seeing a puddle for the first time, I know, but back then this was truly ground breaking stuff - and I HAD to know how to make my designs move like this.

So, I bought a book about coding, took a day off work "sick" (which naturally I don't condone, *ahem*) and learned how to create websites. By the end of the first day, I had created my first site, added animation and interaction, and launched it live - I was so excited! Instantly I saw the potential in this - now every business, however small, could compete on a truly level playing field with the big guys. I could make a one-man-band look like an orchestra! EVERYONE was going to want this; my new career was born!!!

Off I went to see my boss and tell him how we *had* to get a website out there and I was the perfect (read "only") person in the Company to do this. He told me the internet was a "passing phase" but if I wanted to have a go I could - so my first commercial website was born. (With delicious irony, his Company is now a client of mine and I remind him of his initial view of the internet from time to time, just for fun.) I went on to design and create websites during those early web design boom years for many local companies, charities and government agencies - before being snapped up to form a new web department for a local design agency, training their traditional designers to think of screens not paper as the company (like so many others) scrambled to "cash in" on the web design market.

Trouble is that by now I saw more and more of that "cashing in", watching unsuspecting business owners spend *thousands* on super basic sites that either looked great but didn't work, or looked awful but functioned perfectly - neither of which were serving the businesses commissioning them who were desperate to grow their reach, enquires and impact through this amazing new platform. There seemed to be no bridge between the programmers who could code but didn't care how it looked or the designers who made it look amazing until you pressed a button and nothing happened - and that was before you reached the point of how to keep the site live, be found easily, reach new customers, etc...

I decided to <u>be</u> the answer I couldn't find - to create a company staffed by great designers who were not asked to code and great coders who were not asked to design - instead everyone just did the thing they were terrific at and loved doing, or "each to their own" as my Dad always used to say! Soon we were creating fantastic looking sites that actually worked AND met the real needs of ambitious business owners who were tired of hearing "you must have ABC..." or "you really need an XYZ..." - when these gimmicks didn't suit them or appeal to their target audience. Putting the target audience first became what we were known for, as we really took the time to understand the needs of the website *visitor*, while diplomatically guiding the business owner on how their own personal tastes may not best serve them ;-)

Of course, as our client base expanded, we needed people on the team who knew about search engines, choosing a good domain name, how to expand or promote the site, etc and, as everything we create is bespoke and tailor-made to the individual needs of each business, this takes time and these were not "pile them high, sell them cheap" websites. There were, however, commonalities. Certain "ingredients" if you will, which we saw crop up time and again in the most successful sites we built. These traits and focus points worked time and again for *every* type of business - from pants to paintings - all we had to do was cherry-pick the right ones for the job and put them in the right order. This was too good to keep to myself, so I committed there and then to pinpointing each and every element required to make a website that could *really* make a difference for a business, and help business owners grow rapidly from six figures to seven and beyond.

That was the basis of my Website Mastery Method - a unique five step process which covers the essential ingredients for a successful website, from initial idea to a self-supporting promotional machine for your business. I've spent the last 20+ years refining, updating and perfecting this system, and now know that with every element in place, it <u>will</u> deliver the elegant, engaging and effective web solution to meet and exceed your goals.

This book gives you an invaluable blueprint, a recipe to follow and questions to ask yourself along the way which aim to reconnect you with *why* you started your business in the first place. Rediscover the love you have for the customers you want to serve, those *dream* clients you really enjoy working with and *know* you get great results for time and time again. One of the first questions I ask my clients "who do you *want* to work with?" - because <u>that</u> is who your website is all about. Let's get you started on your journey to deliver a great online experience which will attract, engage and capture the attention of those dream clients of yours - in huge numbers - with surprising speed.

You hold this in your hands and I am here to walk you through it every step of the way.

LET'S BEGIN :-)

WHAT TO KNOW BEFORE WE DIVE IN

STRATEGY FIRST
= MEASURABLE RESULTS LATER

I've had the great privilege to work with countless six-figure business owners who've wasted good money on bad websites before they came to me so, if this sounds like you, you are not alone. Moreover, you're not stupid for believing someone who told you they could deliver the results you want - *BUT* <u>if you are honest with yourself</u>, were you *super* clear on what those results actually were?

At this point in a face-to-face conversation, I usually pause for the explosion, outrage, denials - sometime even expletives - then when the dust settles, I ask it again.

WHY? TWO REASONS:

Number one: if you can't *specifically* say what the results are that you're seeking, you have literally no way of ever knowing if you've achieved them. The key here is *specific*. When you say you want "more traffic" - how much more? One extra person a day technically meets this directive, but it's not going to help you grow your business - so what will? Ten? One hundred? Ten thousand? Time and again I've heard business owners lament the "failure" of a website achieving thousands of visitors a day - only to discover that their true opinion of success is the number of sales / downloads / signups / etc - perhaps without ever having shared this with their team or the person trying to hit a moving target of a goal for a website with no strategy behind it. A game of football with no goal at either end would be a long and uninspiring event, your website build should be anything but this.

The second reason I ask this question is for those visionaries, creatives and innovators out there who really want a website to launch their brand to a global audience but tend to have 20 new ideas each day before breakfast! If this sounds familiar to you, it may follow that you have a tendency to go off at a tangent midway through a project (justifiably so, as you have just had the world's greatest idea...), meaning the project runs over time, over budget and somehow becomes diluted in both the message you want to get out there and therefore the impact you can have. I've worked with businesses and organisations from hundreds of industries and various sectors who've been trying to scale up from six figures to seven and beyond, only to become stuck or bump up against a revenue "ceiling", often because projects don't seem to be fully completed before the next has started.

To be clear, there's no judgement here; this is definitely me! It has taken *years* of self-training and building systems around myself to ensure my own projects are completed and launched before I start the next - and it's still a work in progress! For your website however, setting out a clear goal, with a fundamental sequence of steps and actions to follow, will ALWAYS deliver a better result than the "hit and hope" approach. I often liken building a successful website with building a new house. You can have great building materials, building location, the best construction team; but if you don't have architectural plans to follow - and refer back to often - you're never going to achieve that dream home you set out to create.

Strategy First wins every time. I've seen great-looking websites returning terrible results for the business and owners baffled by this. I begin by looking at Strategy First and within 6 months they've delivered SEVEN times the revenue they were before - without looking markedly different! However, you plan to use this book (jumping straight to the chapters which appeal to you most), I cannot recommend highly enough that you start with Strategy First. Your business will thank you for it.

WHAT MAKES THIS DIFFERENT FROM OTHER "BUILD YOUR OWN WEBSITE" BOOKS?

Firstly, there's no coding! When I first started out in the website design and development industry, I wasted hundreds of pounds on books claiming to teach me any number of coding languages within 24 hours - only for that coding language to be obsolete by the time I actually finished the book some years later! Such books are created to support those at the coalface of web development, those whose only concern is to complete six pages by Friday.

What to know before we dive in

YOUR VISION IS BIGGER

You are here to have a massive impact, disrupt your industry, change the world. You're here to guide the process and course-correct it as it glides smoothly to the result you have clearly identified (and conveyed to your team) that will take your business to seven figures and beyond. You're probably not a coder (though you may be, looking for ways to expand what you offer your clients beyond basic code), so I'm not going to try and teach you one's and zero's or show screen grabs that look like the Matrix.

Working with our clients, our core value of Stay in Service always holds true. For most, this means not bombarding them with jargon or hashtag-speak, but translating *their* needs into an online solution. That said, I have included some real gems around the structure and content you'll want to include to get great results from your website and you'll see this highlighted and broken out of the main text - along with real-world examples of how I've seen these actions implemented successfully by a huge number of Companies across the world. Learning from them (regardless of how different your industry is to theirs), *will* benefit you and your online brand, I know this to be true.

IF YOU DON'T YET HAVE A SIX-FIGURE BUSINESS

If you haven't yet achieved a turnover figure of £100k+ per year, many of the principles and structure I suggest in this book will still benefit you, even if you don't yet have the infrastructure I reference here and there - just don't try and eat the pie all at once! Start with Strategy First (get used to hearing me say that!) and set out a goal for your website for one year from today. Break that down into quarterly chunks and actions you can take, then dedicate time in your schedule to work through these - if something I want to do is not in my calendar, it just doesn't happen. Take advantage of the free resources and downloads from my website at www.websitemasterybook.com - where you'll find free helpful workbooks, case studies to inspire you and links to a whole YouTube channel stuffed with great free content and 2-minute tips that you can start applying to your website *today* and start seeing a difference. Once you've got the bug that way, you can revisit this book and get stuck into some of the meatier actions you can take.

As always, sing out if you get stuck - you can book a discovery call on my site and let's have a chat to get you unstuck and into action.

STAGE 1
STRATEGY

CHAPTER 1

WHY DO YOU DO IT?

MISSION. PASSION. PURPOSE. USP.

All synonyms used by marketeers and advertisers in an attempt to instil in their audience a feeling that they're not buying a product or service – they're joining a *cause*.

Sounds a lot more exciting, doesn't it? Having a bigger vision or aim for your business is not only motivating for you and your team, but also appeals to potential clients who will be naturally drawn to your ethos and values – plus it makes you <u>memorable</u>. **So how do you identify and articulate exactly what that is?**

START WITH WHY

Simon Sinek fans (or those who've ever worked with a business coach) will be familiar with his concept of the Golden Circle – a fascinating formula that explains the psychology of nurturing this sense of belonging (also described by Seth Godin as being part of a Tribe), by starting with *why* you do what you do, on the understanding that this appeals far more than *what* you actually do / deliver / create. He explains that this establishes shared values and beliefs, leading to your being trusted more quickly <u>and</u> potentially considered for additional services, products and purchases – as well as encouraging loyalty and long-term custom.

BUT DOES IT MATTER?

Well, yes – with experts estimating **it is ten times more work and effort to attract a new client than to resell to an existing one,** this is something every business hopes to achieve. That's a no-brainer but, as I expand upon later in this book, the importance of your online branding being aligned with your Company values and ethos cannot be underestimated. Failure to *expand* on your message to include the meaning and big picture *mission* behind it may just be what causes your name to fade back into the crowd, instead of standing proud and being chosen.

OKAY, WHERE DO WE START?

To coin a phrase – at the very beginning. Think back to those early days in your business – or before that, when this was all just a twinkle in your eye – what <u>exactly</u> was it that you set out to do? What was that key moment or event when you suddenly thought "hang on, if we did it *this way*, it would be SO much better!" – your Eureka moment if you will? Perhaps it was something you were repelled *from* rather than *toward* which brought you up short and realising *someone* had to do this differently, and it may as well be you?

For me, it was the moment **I realised my love of technology did NOT mean selling website bells and whistles to people who just didn't need them.**

It was the very start of 2001 and design agencies all over the world were stampeding to ride the wave of this new marketing phenomenon "the internet", and to someone like me – creative thinker who can't draw for toffee – this blend of art and technology was a godsend. I was drafted into several organisations to setup their first foray into the world of websites, including agencies keen to cash in on the trend – and *that* is where it started to feel, well, a bit *icky*.

One day I find myself in front of a very nice man (let's call him Jerry), who has shared with me his hopes and plans for his business, how it will support his family, all the good stuff that reminds us why what we do matters. Holding a piece of paper aloft, he says to me "I have this quote from your boss. I've never met him, but feel you get what I'm trying to do in my business, so if *you* tell me that spending..." <insert ridiculous amount of money here!> "... is going to help me do that, I'll do it."

Well. I know what I was *supposed* to say. I know what my boss would have *wanted* me to say. But I just couldn't do it.

You see, Jerry's business was in very early stages and things weren't yet taking off for him so spending the equivalent of a new truck on a website filled with bells and whistles he didn't need – elaborate effects, animation and *soundtrack* (it was the noughties) was

NOT the best investment for his business at that time – and I had to be honest and tell him so. I went back to the office and quit – vowing to only <u>ever</u> propose website solutions that *really* deliver results and meet the *real* needs and objectives of the client.

WHAT DOES THIS HAVE TO DO WITH *YOUR* WEBSITE RIGHT NOW?

There was a <u>reason</u> you started your business, charity or project – and it wasn't about the money. It was something deeper, it was your calling to help a specific person in a specific situation. Remember who that was and the challenge they were facing that you just <u>knew</u> you could help them overcome.

Now write a description of that person in as much details as you can – where they live, their job title, their age group, how much time they have, how much access to budget decisions they have, what would really help them most right now. This is your Ideal Client profile, and helping them to be everything they want to be will form the basis of everything your website is built upon. Share this with the world and your Company will attract *exactly* the sort of clients you want to work with AND stand head and shoulders above the rest.

CHAPTER 2

MORE THAN JUST A PRETTY FACE?

IT'S NEVER GOING TO BE ABOUT HOW PRETTY YOUR WEBSITE LOOKS.

You see, an *effective* site isn't about the number of visitors it attracts, it's about the *revenue generated for your business.*

And I'm afraid only you know what that needs to be – what you will see in six months' time that makes it all worth it – and that means you have some homework to do before you begin.

SO, WHO LIKES MATHS?
NOBODY...?

I don't, I'll admit that, but if you're having a new website built (or you're unhappy with the website you have), it all comes down to the numbers - how else can you measure the return on your investment in a new site?

I know this is true because I've heard so many clients say, 'well, I'll know if I like it'. Or, 'I'll know if lots of people go to it' but (without being too brutal about it), if the till's not ringing, is it making the difference that you wanted it to? And if you don't know <u>before</u> you set out on the journey just where you're trying to get to - you'll never know if you've reached your destination.

IT'S THE SAME WITH YOUR WEBSITE

Just think how great it will be when you look at your books and think "That site has already paid for itself - everything after this point is a bonus!"

So how DO you identify exactly what you'd like your website to achieve in the first place? I'll give you a lovely, super easy formula:

1. You think of a good client – not necessarily the ultimate dream client who's going to walk in with a million pounds in their pocket, but a good client for you. What's the <u>value</u> of that good client?

2. Next look at your current website, the number of visits that you get.

It's important to count <u>visits</u> - that's people, not hits. Hits is a whole techie thing that I could really bore you with, but I'll try not to. You want visits - the number of real people coming to look at your site

---

3. Then the kicker; the <u>conversion</u> rate. How many people visiting your site actually purchase, make an inquiry, or book a meeting with you? And how many go on to become paying customers? The difference between visiting and purchasing - that's your conversion rate.

Knowing these three figures is incredibly powerful, because they hold the key to knowing just how much you should expect your website to generate in terms of actual income – and that should always be more than you spent on it.

Note: this does not mean "get the cheapest site you can"! It means that figuring out your expectations beforehand will help you truly objectively gauge your new website's success.

For example, take the client we worked with who had a successful ecommerce site – but it wasn't as successful as they thought it would be. We took the time to find out the Visit number, the Value number and the Conversion number and they were all pretty good, so what had they expected? One Director instantly replied *"more visitors"* - AT THE EXACT SAME TIME as the other Director said *"more sales"*! Fact was, they hadn't started with a clear picture on either figure, so had no benchmark to measure against, PLUS neither of them had looked at conversion.

Having identified their Visits were high and the Value per sale was within reach of most of those visitors, we could instantly see that Conversion was the issue – with hundreds of visitors to the site each week leaving without making a purchase. Designing and implementing a more engaging user experience for their specific target market and removing obstacles from the purchase process saw their Conversion rate QUADRUPLE within 90 days – more than repaying the cost of the work carried out and going on to ever-increasing sales thereafter.

It <u>can</u> be done, and it's really important to remember that, when you're setting out, don't set *achievable* goals, make them BIG. Let's have some big, fat goals. (Literally, let's have some big, **FAT** goals!) Because you deserve a solution that delivers and *exceeds* the goals that you've set. If you'd like to find out more, please reach out to me at www.websitemasterybook.com and book a free strategy session, so we can find out how we can really get the till ringing and give you a website you love - not just for the looks, but the brains behind it and the difference it makes for your business.

CHAPTER 3

WHY YOUR WEBSITE NEEDS A ROADMAP

YOU KNOW WHAT YOU WANT YOUR WEBSITE TO SAY

You know what you want it to achieve for your business or charity. You know who you want it to appeal to. One thing you may not know is the vital ingredient to bring all of those things together - and that is *flow.*

That word can be pretty polarising, so I don't use it lightly. It may give you flashbacks to the days when business strategists LOVED a flowchart, to *"map your client journey"* or *"chart the lifecycle of your client"* - but these old adages did hold one grain of truth and that is that we human beings (in general) like a path to follow, and your website plays a huge part in that.

In fact, in a large-scale usability study, The Nielsen Norman Group (who host conferences on research-based user experience), cite "**unexpected locations for content**" as the **NUMBER ONE** most **damaging mistake you can make on your website.** In simple terms, that means people visiting your website just cannot find what they're looking for - because there's no flow. No clear path through the site or in the way information on your site is structured.

To help you put this in context, let's compare an ecommerce site with a bricks and mortar retail shop. Imagine you walk into a shop on your High Street and start making your way down the aisle, only to find a dead end? You have to turn around and go back on yourself, you're almost back to the door you entered through when you spot another aisle and head off down that one, to find that it splits in two and you've no idea which to choose as there's no signage or obvious clear path.

YOU WOULDN'T STAY VERY LONG OR BUY VERY MUCH, WOULD YOU?

It's the same on your website. Your aim is for your target audience to arrive on your site, read wording that speaks directly to them and the reason they came to you and make it BLATANTLY obvious from the outset exactly which next step they should take, which button to click or which page you've created specifically to meet their needs. The result? **They feel comfortable with you, think you understand them and what they're looking for, they feel safe in your hands.**

Give them the "dead end" routine or (heaven forbid) expect them to figure it out as to how to use your site and they'll be lost in more ways than one...

SO HOW DO YOU DESIGN AND ENGINEER A SEAMLESS CUSTOMER JOURNEY - OR FLOW - INTO YOUR WEBSITE?

Start by really understanding your client's needs. Not just what you'd like to show them, but what they came to you to find - it is often a very different thing. Having a clear understanding of your target audience and the way your product or service helps them in their lives is the key here, but then EXPAND your view and include who they are as individuals.

For example, you may be selling a product to young men aged between 18 and 25. You've identified the sort of imagery they like, the right colour scheme, great wording, etc, and know just how to present your product on the page in a way they will like. Now step back and look at that audience - **how did they come to your site?** Which device are they using to access it? How much free time do they have to wander around your site - do they need to get straight to the checkout or do they want lots of information first?

Understanding the journey your customer is on in their mind, before they even reach your site, will help you to map out the route they will prefer once they are IN your site.

One client of ours recently had us redesign and update their website as their target client group had evolved over time and they wanted to attract a slightly different audience. Having identified the profile (or avatar, as it's now popular to say!), for the new audience, we could see that these people were fact-driven, enjoyed free content and liked to do their research before making a decision - but they were often short of time.

We engineered this understanding into the sitemap - the flow for the website - to give short, valuable snippets of information and rapid, direct access to make their enquiry about the packages and programmes specifically designed for their needs. We blended this with readily-available blogs for more detail, which they could return to when they had time - in exchange for their one-step subscription to the mailing list.

As a result, **enquiries are up and the Company mailing list has increased significantly** - ensuring future information will automatically be filtered and sent out to precisely the right audience for each blog post or article created.

Flow is the vital component of your website success plan so don't skip this important stage when first planning your site. **Guide your customer and they won't be lost to you, or your site.**

CHAPTER 4

HOW LONG WILL THIS TAKE?

In over twenty years spent designing websites, there is one question I'm asked on EVERY single project, without exception:

HOW LONG BEFORE WE CAN LAUNCH?

...and the answer is always the same - **how much time do you have?**

"Not a problem", I hear. "I'm ready to go right now" – but that's not always how it ends up happening. You're part of the creative process and you're going to have homework to do! We sometimes find ourselves chasing a client for their wording / images / feedback as we build sites with them - and it always seems to be based in underline. Not reluctance for the site to be finished, but a resistance to the technology involved.

You see, when it comes to my industry, a lot of people are stuck in the belief that they don't *like* technology - and they see that as an obstacle to be overcome - when the truth is, you don't *need* to like tech, just like what it can <u>do for you</u>. Learn to look past the process and embrace the results you'll enjoy and your project will flow smoothly.

SO HOW DO YOU DO THIS?

Start by making a list, simple as that. Create a list of what you would like your website to achieve - dream big and be specific here (see my short video on measuring your Return on Investment at www.youtube.com/@fatpromotions), it doesn't have to be a long list, one or two points will do.

Then list a few key points about your ideal client, who you really want to work with - read Chapter 10 on Designing for Your Ideal Client to help with this. Then the really smart part:

Share this list with your web developer and ask them "What do you need from me?"

I'll give you an example of this in action; a charity we've worked with for several years was started by wonderful lady whose child was clearly suffering from an undiagnosed condition affecting their development. So, this lady has made it her life's work to raise awareness of the condition and how to spot it, to protect any other parent from going through her experience - with enormous success! She now runs a charity to support this and speaks on a world stage of her experience - and the changes her charity have effected in legislation and medical improvements are staggering and inspiring.

BUT SHE *LOATHES* TECHNOLOGY

Hates it. Barely uses a mobile phone if she can avoid it - so where to begin when tasked with creating a website to reach the millions of parents across the world who need to hear her message? On top of this, she was concerned about the time involved in the project and feared she "may hold it up" as her time was so limited.

This is where great planning really saves the day. Every project we work on starts with two things:

1. A list of what we'll need from you to get the job done
2. A schedule right at the start so you know <u>when</u> we're going to need it!

Having provided our client with both of these things, and working closely together to coordinate the time she had available, we were able to give a clear schedule for the project from start to finish - including any milestones and key points when we'd require her input so she could plan ahead and didn't feel overwhelmed by the process. Her website saw an increase in awareness and volunteer signups went from 1 or 2 a month to over 20 per week as a result!

Every client (or prospective client) I speak with asks me how long it will take - and tell me they can move as fast as we do. My advice is to be fully aware of what you want to achieve <u>first</u>, then we work with you to reverse engineer this into what you need from us, and when we'll all see the results.

Because then it comes to your website build, we will always hold your hand, but we can't do your homework 😊.

CHAPTER 5

WE COMPETE FOR ATTENTION, BUT WE'RE NOT COMPETITORS

- HOW DOES THAT WORK?

If you and I both want to work with the same person, we must be competitors, right? Wrong.

SO, WHEN IS YOUR COMPETITION NOT YOUR COMPETITION?

Have you ever turned up to a networking event, whether it's online or (back in the old days!) face-to-face, and found yourself talking to somebody who does the same thing you do? Very often you think, *'I'm wasting my time. I need to move on to someone else'* (unless they're just a particularly nice person you want to have a chat with). But if you're there for business, chances are you're competing, right?

Now, let's change that and re-frame it to working with your website…

If you're aiming at a particular type of client, a great tip is to look at what other websites are doing who <u>aren't</u> competing with you, but who <u>also aim at that type of client</u>.

I'LL GIVE YOU AN EXAMPLE:

We created a website for a large UK company, who run a number of care homes and nursing homes, offering very specialist care. The first thing we do at FAT Promotions with every project we handle, is we do a project compass. This is our blueprint - a unique document that we create for every project we work on and it gives a full 360-degree view of your business website, answering the following:

- Who's looking at it?
- Who's looking for you?
- Who's <u>not</u> looking for you who *could* be?

Then we look at your competitors. This may sound like a weird thing to do because we're not just going to copy what they do *(all we know is we're going to make your website look better than theirs!)*, but what we're actually looking at is **who** is looking at those competitors - and are they finding what they want?

That's especially useful if we're looking at others in the same industry as you - but who else should you consider?

With the care homes and nursing homes, we worked with their in-house marketing team to identify that their target audience was not the senior people themselves who chose the home, but usually their sons and daughters, who tended to be in their forties, early fifties.

The key question to ask was:
What else are <u>those</u> people looking at?

What else were they looking at during the same time that they're looking for possible care for their loved ones? And the answer was... estate agents! Their choice was actually between finding the best possible long-term care provisions OR moving to a larger house and have their mum/dad come and live with them. So, we looked at estate agent sites, and the first thing that anybody looks for is *'where do you want to go?'*

We realised that was the key message to get across. When someone was looking at our clients for nursing and long-term care provision, it wasn't about how pretty it looked or the care services they offered or how big they were. It was: **where are you?** Because they didn't want to waste time reviewing a care home in Glasgow if they lived in Cornwall!

It all came down to location. That was all that mattered to that target client.

This is the key thing to consider when you are creating your website and thinking, *'who is going to be using this?'* Try expanding that, and ask yourself:

- What else are they looking at?
- Who else is competing for their attention, but they're not competing with you?

By asking these questions, you can gain a real insight into **how to get a much better conversion rate for your website** (and therefore return on your investment) than you would otherwise achieve.

CHECKPOINT: STAGE 1

CONGRATULATIONS – WE HAVE REACHED THE END OF STAGE 1: STRATEGY!

For some people, this stage lights them up – planning ahead, setting goals, sharing their vision – for others it can feel like having to read the rules before you can play the game. Whichever category you fall in to, I promise you this: time spent in this stage is *never* wasted. Think of this as gathering all of the components needed to build the very vessel to take your business to stratospheric heights!

To give you an easy recap / checklist of the key elements mentioned in this stage, in case you missed them:

- **Ideal client profile:**
  - What do they like, where to reach them, who are the similar but non-competing sites
- **Return on investment:**
  - What's the value of good client, what are the numbers for your current site performance, how to measure the return on your investment
- **Sitemap:**
  - Including all the legal bits, essentials for your own benefit, using wording that appeals to your client profile
- **Schedule:**
  - Planning ahead for content, bringing in strategic partners for photos, copywriting, and other elements you'll need, doing your homework
- **Compass:**
  - Solidify all of the above into a one-page plan, refer to and review this throughout the process, use as blueprint / roadmap for the entire project to stay on course at all times.

If these aren't ringing any bells, go back and review the chapters in this Stage and work through the exercise in each one. You'll want them ALL in your toolkit before we move on to the next stage.

Struggling with this? Strategy dictates the success of your website so if you're a little stuck in getting started, don't worry – reach out and book a quick session with me at www.websitemasterybook.com and let's kick start the process together!

STAGE 2

DESIGN

CHAPTER 6

GOOD THINGS START AT HOME

YOU KNOW YOU WANT YOUR ONLINE PRESENCE TO ATTRACT THE RIGHT TYPE OF CLIENT AND DELIVER REAL RESULTS

That means more than a one-page website. But is that what you (effectively) have right now?

If you don't get your homepage right, up to 70% of your website visitors will instantly click away from your site and all that hard work (and "fascinating detail"!) you spent time putting into the rest of your web pages will never be seen. Get it right and those visitors could become the long-term, loyal customers and supporters you deserve.

Think of it as "kerb appeal" for your online showroom!

It's easy to be too close to your own business (and as a proud workaholic, I should know!), but sometimes you need to step back and get a fresh pair of eyes of what you had planned for your website homepage. After all, this is still the single most popular page on every one of the thousands of websites we've built over the last nineteen years - without exception. As a rule, it is always the business owner who knows their product or service better than anyone else - but does that make you the best judge of what your customer *really* wants?

When all's said and done, do you want a homepage <u>you</u> love or which gets the phone / till ringing? The former may give you a warm, fuzzy feeling, but with the latter you can focus on growing and scaling your business - **as big as you want to go.**

A couple of years ago I met a fantastic couple running an established ecommerce business, selling mid-range designer goods online. Lovely people; she was the creative genius and he was the pragmatic integrator every business needs, they sold a quality product and website visitor numbers were high. Yet their conversion rate (moving visitors to the "paying customer" bracket) was a painfully low 4% - just not enough to fund the plans they had to expand and free up some of their precious time currently spent "working on the website" every day.

They got there by focusing purely on the numbers, not on what their customers *wanted*. This resulted in the wrong sort of customers coming to the site, and the right sort leaving when they did.

I had to share that painful truth of every website - it's not about you!

Having really got to know who they wanted to attract, and who was most likely to buy their fabulous products, my team came up with a new design which appealed to these dream customers *on their level*. It featured the sort of engaging content and styling they like, gave styling tips and ideas (just by changing the way the original content was presented - no extra work required), and joined up the website with their efforts on social media for a fully integrated approach.

Conversion **increased from 4% to 16% within 90 days,** and that was *after* putting a pause on their paid advertising elsewhere, saving them literally thousands of pounds. Win win!

If you've been telling yourself your website would work harder if only more people saw it... Stop. Go back to the kerb and take a good, hard look at your homepage and what it promises your customers - because that's who it's all about.

CHAPTER 7

IS YOUR WEBSITE DESIGN READY TO GO GLOBAL?

YOU MAY (OR MAY NOT) KNOW THAT THE "WWW" AT THE START OF YOUR COMPANY WEBSITE STANDS FOR WORLD WIDE WEB BUT, IF YOU DO, YOU MAY THINK THAT'S ALL THE "GLOBAL" THINKING YOU NEED.

After all, the beauty of the internet is that your site can be seen by the whole world BUT does your site feature global *thinking*?

I'm not talking about "aiming high" or planning for world domination (cue nefarious laugh in the style of a Bond villain!), but the elements or features of your site which will appear in multiple places. To the technical among us, these are referred to as "global elements" and they can make all the difference to the success of your website.

As an example, how many times have you visited a website homepage and experienced a simple, few-choices menu bar to access the remaining pages of the site - only to find that clicking through to one of those pages then delivers a completely different looking menu that leaves you lost? Or perhaps you're using a site and about to click a button that said "order now" on the previous page, but this had suddenly changed to "enquire now"? What happened there?

The truth is, it is SOOOOO easy to lose a customer or potential sale from your site simply through a lack of consistency. Human beings are creatures of habit, with most of us favouring the well-known names (and websites) we trust and have visited before. This presents your new website with numerous challenges as you battle to reach the top of the pile, but it all boils down to one fundamental thing - building familiarity FAST!

AND THE KEY TO *THAT* IS A SMOOTH, CONSISTENT JOURNEY THROUGH YOUR WEBSITE

I've written before about the importance of ease of navigation so you don't lose people on their way through your site (revisit Chapter 3 on this), which all comes down to your site's structure, but the *design* plays a separate and equally important role in this. Changes between navigation menus, text sizes, even colour choices - all of these can disorientate a visitor quickly, and that never ends well. Making sure your call to action is easily recognisable regardless of which page it appears on is a basic, but you can also control the size, position and style of your images so they all match on every page - anything that protects your website visitor from the "jarring" experience of a sudden change is vital to make them feel right at home, and therefore ready to engage with your products or services.

But manually checking each and every one of these things on every single page of your website will take you FOREVER!!!

Welcome to Global Elements. Global Elements are chunks of re-usable code which you know will always look exactly as you want them too, regardless of which page they appear on. These tiny blueprints can control the fonts, colours, spacing, styling, position, etc of those elements and the beauty is you can edit them in ONE PLACE and have the entire website instantly updated to match this. Nice, eh? You want a newsletter signup box with blue text and a link to your Privacy Policy added to ten different pages scattered throughout your website? Done. You want to change blue text to pink and have every one of those boxes update automatically? Easy peasy. How about adding that same box to some additional pages in your site without having to recode them all over again? Not a problem. By creating one central library of the little features and widgets your site contains, you just became more consistent AND more *scalable* - vital to your website's *manageable* future growth.

This was exactly the challenge faced by an international charity who came to us with a website that had outgrown the original incarnation and suffered from bits and pieces being added "here and there" as the organisation grew. When carrying out our website audit (to identify all issues including technical, security and usability), we discovered that their main navigation menu was not coded as a global element, but was independently added to each page of the site. As a result, it appeared in wildly varying versions on different pages with some links missing altogether! This not only caused frustration to the in-house team trying to manage the site, but rendered the site barely usable for the public visitor.

We corrected this by identifying the global elements - which elements (such as page navigation menus) needed to appear consistently throughout the site. The difference has been phenomenal! Not only is the site easier to use and makes it far easier to access all of their great content, the maintenance hours required to keep the site updated has been drastically reduced now that any site-wide changes can be carried out easily in one central place.

When planning your website, take the time to consider which bits you'd like to see on every page / some pages / particular sections. Be this the position of the links to other pages, the style of the buttons you want users to click, or that familiar "Ready to contact us?" Enquiry block - they can all be controlled by global elements and save you valuable time (and money) as your Company website evolves. And that's a whole new wwworld ;-)

Further insights can be found in my Website Insight Video Series on our YouTube channel at www.youtube.com/@fatpromotions, including:

How colour choices on your website could half your audience

Create a compelling call to action, for website success

CHAPTER 8

WITHOUT BRAND VALUES, WHO WILL VALUE YOUR BRAND?

DID YOU KNOW THAT "BRANDING" IS ACTUALLY A REALLY NEGATIVE WORD?

If you look it up in the thesaurus, you get the instant results of:

- Stigmatise
- Taint
- Disgrace
- Mark

...they're all pretty depressing.

Yet in the business world we all think of branding as a positive thing, as how you represent your company in your brochures / your logo / in the business cards currently languishing on your desk (!) - and, of course, as the way your company is represented by your website. It's no wonder talking about their branding makes so many business owners I know feel icky when you realise it has such negative connotations at a root level.

One thing you might not know is that getting your branding wrong can be the absolute killer for your website - particularly in the current climate. Fact is that right now (maybe more than ever), you need to feel sure that your branding is a positive message that clearly sends your message out to the world AND clearly expresses your *values* as a business.

Looking at the statistics, according to Small Biz Genius Industry Insights, **89% of shoppers stay loyal to brands that share their values.** And right now, although things are tight financially in the economy worldwide, finding a company whose values match your own is seriously attractive to the customer.

So, getting your branding right means far more than making sure your colours and fonts all match - it's making sure that how you look online is congruent with who you are as a Company. If you value always being trustworthy and reliable in the real world, your website needs to reflect that. Get it right, and potential customers resonate with your message, your values and your ethos, then they're *naturally* drawn to you - you've built trust for your business through your website before you've even met. And that turns a visitor to your website into a customer.

Get it wrong, fail to get your values across clearly (or worse, give out the wrong message entirely), and you've lost more than a sale.

I can speak from recent experience about this as this is something we've done a lot of work on in the FAT team in the last few months. It's been a good time to reflect on what our values are and what we stand for. As a team, we sat down and worked through an exercise to help us collectively agree on our core values - what do we really stand for, and what will we not stand for, as a team.

It's essential to work this out as a team - even if you only have two staff - because it's important to get everyone behind it.

Having agreed on what our core values are, we're now applying them across all our marketing material and promotion (i.e. our Branding), to share them with the world. If you're interested, our core values are defined as:

Start in service - we are responsible trustworthy and approachable at all times

Always learning - committed to improving and growing as individuals and as a team

Process driven - to maintain our high standards or accuracy and our organised approach

Embrace a challenge - we're hard working, tenacious and we show up

Bigger thinking - always adding value, generating new ideas and innovating as we go.

Having set that out in our own company vision, it's now important that we update our website to reflect these values because, just as you wouldn't hand out a business card with out-of-date details, your website should always reflect who you are right now, and what you stand for. That in itself attracts the right sort of customers you want to work with.

We had a great example of this recently when the owner of an established company approached us for a new site about their professional services. They could demonstrate excellence in their particular service industry, but when they spoke about it, they were very good at focussing on telling stories of how people got it wrong because they hadn't known what they were doing, because they were making foolish mistakes. We sat down with them as part of the initial strategy stage of their website build (step one of our Website Mastery Method, as you now know!) and asked what their values are, why do they do what they do, what do they love about it? They lit up when they spoke of how they loved to take the hard work off their customers' plate and handle all of the compliance paperwork for them, saving them time and giving peace of mind. Those are their company values and that's exactly what the new website will lead with - *automatically* attracting people who already resonate with that message, as well as needing the services they provide.

Make sure your branding doesn't just coordinate with your existing promotional materials, but reflects your ethos and values. That will attract customers with the *same* ethos and values, and that's *exactly* the sort of customer you want to work with. If this is something you're struggling with, reach out to me and have a free discovery call or a strategy session so we can get you on track, clarify your message, and make sure it's represented beautifully on your website. Because we do websites, it's all we do and we do it really, really well.

CHAPTER 9

GOOD AT WHAT YOU DO? PROVE IT!

IF I ASK YOU HOW GOOD YOU *REALLY* ARE AT WHAT YOU DO, YOU'RE GOING TO TELL ME YOU'RE THE BEST - RIGHT?

(If not, you may have just found why your conversion rate is low - everyone loves a confident reply!) But if I asked you to *prove* this, would you know where to start?

There's a popular term doing the rounds now and that is Social Proof - which means it's not about how good **you** say you are, it's all about what **other** people are saying about you - and that means in <u>public</u>.

Go to 90% of websites and you'll find a Testimonials page - a list of all the happy clients that company has served over the years and how super happy they are with everything that's been done for them. However, look behind the scenes at your website visitor traffic - not just how many people view the page but how long they stay on it - and you'll see first-hand what I can tell you from my own experience hosting thousands of active websites over the last twenty years through our own hosting service - ***nobody reads your Testimonials page!***

They may read the first one or two if they're not too long, but a whole page? Nobody has time for that AND they may start to doubt the origin of these - however genuine they may be - because they're coming from **you**. If these appear on your own site, promoting your products or services, it's all too easy for potential customers to wonder how unbiased and genuine they may be - and that destroys *trust*.

When it comes to your website (whether you're a business, solopreneur or charity), the number one goal **must** be to establish credibility and trust - and quickly - because without that the sale can stop dead. Get this right, with a few well-balanced quotes from happy clients scattered throughout your website, backed up by external sources, and you're on your way to another sale and another happy customer.

SO HOW DO YOU GO ABOUT IT?

It's easy to think Social Proof means what people read on your own social media channels - your business description on Facebook or your LinkedIn bio - but that's not your only option. Of course, we always recommend our clients reach out on a regular and recurring basis to customers of theirs to request reviews on Google and Facebook directly, or ask to be recommended on LinkedIn - but there are many *other* ways to build your reputation for new clients coming to you for the first time and the key ones are **Association, Accreditation** and **Certification.**
Feature badges, icons and links for these in the footer of your website and you could be building stronger foundations than you realise.

These could be for well known, reputable third-party review sites for your industry who list or feature your Company - TripAdvisor if your business is in hospitality is a great example of this, as is Check-A-Trade for tradespeople and construction companies. Through third party sites like this, customers can leave direct, impartial and *honest* reviews of their experience with your service, so people are more likely to trust them and trust **you** as you're confident to link to these and share them.

If you're involved in the financial or law sectors, you'll have your own governing bodies and guidelines to adhere to - don't be afraid to display these icons, qualifications and accreditations and exploit this as another way to evidence how good you are and how this has been recognised.

BUT WHAT IF THERE IS NO INDUSTRY-SPECIFIC ACCREDITATION FOR WHAT YOU DO?

This is where your *credibility* comes in. By proudly displaying that you're a member or registered affiliate of a known and trusted organisation, potential customers can see you as trustworthy by *association*. After all, a national business group serving members all over the UK and a renowned campaigning body for the benefit of the business economy, wouldn't accept a business who acted in a non-integrous way, surely? Or, if the latter <u>did</u> occur, the customer feels they have an avenue through which to address this - that little bit of **additional reassurance** to help them make the important decision to work with you.

We guided a specialist consultant to do exactly this with his brand-new website and saw the results *fast*. Despite years of experience in his niche and specialist field, as a new business in his own right he did not yet have a bank of happy customers to call upon and offer reassurance to potential new clients with testimonials and case studies on his site. Instead, we found out which professional bodies he belonged to; which networking groups; which documents and certifications he had to support his position as a trusted, reliable business. Once he started to think about it, he came up with almost 10 different ones for us to add to his new website - along with logos and links to each for full transparency *plus* building reciprocal links for search engine visibility.

THE RESULT? INSTANT CREDIBILITY!

Just displaying these on his new site showed the world he is a "proper business" - someone taking their responsibility seriously and committed to the long-term service and commitment his potential customers were looking for. Not only did this endear him to private clients, but he received a large public sector enquiry within days of his new website launch as, by displaying his accreditations, he'd already done the initial filtering work *for* them.

If you're really good at what you do, don't wait to be *asked* to prove it. Go out of your way, right from the start, to show the world your business is reliable, credible and trustworthy because **that** is what drives enquiries through a website far faster than any testimonial page ever will.

CHAPTER 10

DESIGN YOUR WEBSITE FOR EVERYONE AND MISS THE ONE YOU WANT

YOU DON'T NEED A WEBSITE THAT APPEALS TO THOUSANDS OF PEOPLE – IT NEED ONLY APPEAL TO ONE PERSON TO BE TRULY SUCCESSFUL.

You just need to know who that person is.

Truth is, this applies to all forms of marketing your business (or raising awareness of your charity / cause / event) and without that <u>clarity</u> of who that is, *you're going to work ten times harder to see real results...*

Fact is, on your website this is the difference between a page view and a paying customer.

Many of us use <u>networking</u> as a method to tell the world about our products and services or the great work we do, right? In 2021 the business community saw exponential growth in online networking for obvious reasons, with all major players in the business community (such as FSB and BNI) maximising the exposure and knowledge-sharing this presented for their members.

Imagine attending a networking event (online or otherwise) and, instead of waiting your turn for 60 seconds or less to explain how great you are at what you do, you just started shouting it into the room? Randomly calling out about what you do to anyone who could hear, in the hope that they *might* want to know more later. *I'm willing to bet your success rate would be painfully low.*

Now instead, picture this; you're sitting across the table from a single person who fits your ideal client profile perfectly and you're having an <u>engaging discussion</u> one to one. **How's that success rate looking now?**

Without a clear message aimed at the one person you <u>really</u> want to work with, that's exactly what your website is missing – and it's blocking your success. Massively.

We all know how vital a clear client profile (sometimes referred to as your client avatar) can be to every piece of marketing and awareness-raising you do, but in your website, it is **everything**.

By understanding who they are, you can determine which devices they use, which browser they favour, which other sites they regularly visit – then apply this *"inside knowledge"* to your site to ensure it appeals to them on their level.

As an example, we recently created a website for a Gym in Bristol who offer online and in-person tailored personal training to a wide client base. Their old site had great photography and adequate traffic but online enquiries were not at the level to support the Company's plans for growth. Getting to know the Company ethos and values, it became clear they had a *specific target client-type,* with a *specific problem* easily solved by the experienced and highly trained team.

The new website was then designed and constructed around this understanding, with images, colour scheme and even font styles carefully selected to **appeal directly to that single client profile** – without alienating anyone else – resulting in not only *attracting higher visitor numbers than ever*, but online enquiries have risen to the point where the Company is now extending their staff team to cope with additional demand.

Whatever your business or organisation does, there is someone out there just waiting to hear your message.

Your website design (not just the visual appeal but also the structure) should *always* have that individual at front of mind from Homepage to Contact and everywhere in between.

That one person could be the difference you're looking for, and they're waiting to hear from <u>you</u>.

CHECKPOINT: STAGE 2

NOW WE'RE MOVING – WE HAVE REACHED THE END OF STAGE 2: DESIGN!

Often this is the most popular stage as many of our clients are very visually-driven people – which can be a good thing, but can also trip you up. The mistake I see most often is that it is easy to get caught up in what <u>you</u> like and dislike when (if you recall from the Strategy work you did in Stage 1), your website is not about you – it's about the likes and dislikes of the people you want to work with. Keep their needs front and foremost at this stage.

Here is your recap / checklist of the key elements mentioned in this stage, in case you need to revisit these:

- **Homepage first:**
  - Sets the tone for the whole site, make user-centric, fundamentals to include to connect and engage
- **Inner pages:**
  - Which components will carry through the site, setting your font / colour palette for the project, how do you want people to get in touch – and how to make that easy
- **Branding:**
  - Seamlessly coordinates with your existing marketing, ensure this reflects your ethos and values, expanding upon your message and meaning
- **Success by Association:**
  - Including industry body logos, qualifying your expertise through certifications, build trust with memberships and affiliations

- **Appeal:**
  - o Always refer to your ideal client as you would a friend, design for one person for a clear message, what do your target audience use to view your website

Review the design work / changes you've made over the course of this stage and – if you find you've slipped off the path of user-centric (i.e., it's not your tastes we're playing to) - go back and review the chapters in this Stage and work through the exercise in each one. Spending a little more time here now will save you HOURS later, trust me!

Easy way to gauge the decisions you've made at this stage is to review with a fresh set of eyes – and we don't mean your friends and family! If you want a professional view, reach out and book a quick session with me at www.websitemasterybook.com and I'll be happy to help

---

STAGE 3
CREATION

CHAPTER 11

WHO IS YOUR WEBSITE ACTUALLY ABOUT?

(CLUE: IT'S NOT YOU!)

You see, how many years you've been in business, how many staff you have on your team, how many different products or services you offer: these may make you feel great, but do nothing to build that essential bridge between website visitor and website customer – <u>relationship</u>.

But wait! (I hear you cry) *Surely telling them all of that shows that we are the best choice for them to buy from!*

SADLY NO - UNLESS YOU SPELL IT OUT
FOR THEM

One major trend we've seen in times of tumultuous economy is the customers' hesitation to put their money into anything, unless they can see exactly what's in it for them. If consumer trust is at an all-time low, presenting a potential client with yet another website that pushes facts and figures at them will fail to meet them where they are right now, so my question for you is this: does your website showcase how good you are, or how good you could be <u>for them</u>?

Both are valid as a "shop window", but the latter will lead them inside to find out more and build trust. Without that, they'll simply keep walking...

When I hold a strategy meeting with a potential new client, they often rush to tell me how great their company or service is, of their accolades and achievements, why everyone should buy from them and not from their competitors, etc, etc. I'm naturally a nosy person (!) so this level of details is both fascinating and useful in the plans we form together on how best to convey this online. However, once we have that part "out of the way", the question I always ask is **"and who is your dream customer or client?"**

No longer being nosy, this is the most valuable part, where we learn about what they truly offer and how it changes the lives of the people who come to them, because THEY are who your website is actually for.

FOR EXAMPLE:

- **You say:** we sell jewelled handbags
- **Your website says:** we help women (manbags aside for a second) to look stylish for any occasion
- **You say:** we offer financial advice
- **Your website says:** we help you live the retirement you've dreamed of, starting now

Get the drift? We're showing the outcome, the results, the benefit they find after choosing to work with / buy from you over someone else. And it's not just words, the images you choose for you website can also reflect the positive impact choosing your company can have on their lives.

Like the Mortgage Broker Company we worked with, who specialise in finding solutions for homeowners at all stages of life. We identified that older couples looking for lifetime mortgages (to free up equity in their homes), were really looking for ways to enjoy life more – quite apart from where they chose to live. So, the words and images we chose reflected new found freedoms, travel, luxury purchases they'd not previously allowed themselves. As a result, this target group now forms the majority of enquiries to that website – target found!

If you're struggling to find the words to take your website from good to great, remember it's not about you. It's all about who you want to work with and the results you can give them. That's real service - and ALL customers love that!

CHAPTER 12

IMAGE IS EVERYTHING

IT IS SAID THAT A PICTURE PAINTS A THOUSAND WORDS, SO WHY WOULD YOU USE THE VISUAL EQUIVALENT OF SLANG?

By that I mean poor imagery, particularly on your website where you have less than a handful of seconds to capture someone's attention - see the later chapter regarding online attention span (Crack the Code) for more on that.

A study published by Psychology Today tells us more about the effect taking photos has on future recognition and, therefore, familiarity - something vital when you're trying to build a brand. Making your website a visually pleasing experience can only be a good thing, plus you've already invested in great design, user experience and - of course - your top-quality product or service!

Yet time and again we see sites with poor quality or ill-chosen images which really don't give that warm, fuzzy feeling your dream clients are looking for when they come to your site. Regardless of whether they're looking for your specific product or have been personally referred to your service, **your website is the first port of call for that** *essential* **relationship-building** that must take place to guide them from being a passer-by to a long-term advocate of what you have to offer.

WE KNOW, IT'S ALL ABOUT THE BUDGET!

However, treated properly, investing in great photos for your website can pay for itself over and again - PLUS you can re-purpose the images (subject to agreement with the photographer), into your other marketing materials, posters, banner, business cards, social posts, etc. With high resolution digital versions, you really can "cook once and eat often"!

There are other options for you besides bespoke photographer too. Stock Image libraries have come a long way since the days of flicking through printed brochure, selecting and noting the 12-digit reference numbers and mailing off for a copy of the slide - *I'm giving away my age now, aren't I?*

These days, there are hundreds of high-quality stock libraries online who will let you login, create an account, pay for credits and download exactly the photo you've been looking for, usually at very affordable rates. A word of warning though - always trial the low resolution / watermarked image *before* you buy as sometimes what looks great on the screen, then just doesn't work on the printed dummy visual. You want to try before you buy.

It's not just *where* you get your images either (though one quick caveat, please don't "grab" images from Google and imagine they're copyright free - they almost certainly are not), you need to think about the content and composition too.

Begin by considering:

- **Close-ups - vs - wide-angle shots.** The latter can make a small room look larger; the former can emphasise the little added value touches you deliver

- **People - vs - places.** You may be very proud of your freshly painted dining room, but do all those empty chairs and tables just make your restaurant look empty? Got some great shots of happy smiling customers? Make sure you have their permission to use these in your marketing or apply some stylised editing to blur faces in a crowd.

- **Sell the sizzle, not the steak!** One of my favourite expressions, basically means show the positive outcome of dealing with you, not the issue you address. The current trend of emphasising *pain points* for your customers can work in text, but in images it can make your site a bit, well, depressing.

The latter is particularly important for charities and non-profits as donators and funding bodies want to see the wonderful, positive impact of what you do - how you're changing the world through your efforts.

When we worked with one charity tackling homelessness, the first thing we addressed was their imagery. Moving this away from people sleeping on cold streets - whilst handling the sensitivities of their service-users not wishing to be photographed - we instead developed a theme for imagery on their site which reflected the warm and caring welcome given to all. My team then carefully curated the images selected from our vast royalty-free stock libraries, to deliver a serious message in an embracing and collaborative way.

In an age when social media dictates the seemingly "essential" need to look good as individuals, **make sure your organisation stands proud online and represents you authentically, elegantly and, above all, with integrity.**

CHAPTER 13

DO YOU NEED A LAWYER TO BUILD YOUR WEBSITE?

WITH ALL THE TALK OF "INDUSTRY STANDARDS" AND "BEST PRACTICE", HOW DO YOU *REALLY* KNOW WHAT TO INCLUDE ON YOUR WEBSITE?

Which elements are nice / necessary / neither?

There is so much to consider when creating an online presence for your business, charity or organisation; including imagery to choose, words to write, how to explain what it is you do in the 3.2 seconds you have before the visitor clicks away... it's little wonder some of those pesky legal requirements or recommendations may slip your mind.

From GDPR to Distance Selling Regulations - there is a HUGE amount to consider, and you just don't have time to think about that stuff, you have a website to launch, promote and measure your return on investment, right?

But what happens when the Information Commissioners Office come calling? With fines in the UK of up to 4% of your global turnover for failures to meet GDPR requirements - the extra hour it would have taken to sort out that Privacy Policy may just have been worth it after all.

AND WE'RE NOT JUST TALKING DATA PROTECTION...

There are a raft of other considerations to make when creating or upgrading your website too. Basics such as Company name and registered office should be a given, but you can not only offer extra value by adding more information to your website - did you realise you can even make it easier to be *paid* by sharing the important stuff openly and transparently?

Truth is, it does take that little bit of extra effort to build a relationship with your potential customers through your website alone - by which I'm referring to the run-of-the-mill, who-what-why-where-how websites out there - and if you miss this, you're missing a real gem. Instead of a site which talks only about your services plus the bare bones, absolute essentials of Privacy Policy, Cookie Policy, etc - what if you maximised this opportunity to tell your customers more about who you are as an organisation?

LET'S TAKE OPTING IN TO YOUR MAILING LIST AS AN EXAMPLE:

Now, you do have to make clear to the potential customer as they sign up to receive your newsletter, exactly what they're signing up to and with whom - as well as the methods you offer to update them by so they can opt in or out of email / postal / telephone communications.

But instead of saying "Completion of this form adds you to our mailing list...", why not try "We would love to send you discount codes, sneak previews and insider tips - no more than once a month - and we promise to never ever pester you again if you click to unsubscribe at any time. Though we will miss you!"

See how much more friendly and beguiling the second option can be to a potential subscriber - and therefore future customer? It doesn't have to be that casual obviously, tailor this to suit your target audience / industry so the messaging appeals directly to them - read Chapter 10 on identifying your target audience if you need support in this.

Same with ecommerce if you sell goods or services via your website - there are a number of legal requirements to include for this specific area, and potentially more depending on where in the world you're selling to. Yet, instead of a cold, clinical "Returns Policy" page with a basic bulleted list of all the legal nasty necessities - imagine instead offering a page which starts with a great statistic of the number of happy customers served this month, a testimonial or positive review (preferably on a third party site, read the Chapter on Social Proof for support with this), and a personal message from your CEO saying how proud she / he is of the products they sell and how confident they are that you'll be delighted with your purchase that they offer a "no quibble" refund policy on any goods returned unused within XYZ days....etc?

THINK HOW COMPELLING THAT IS WHEN CHOOSING TO HIT THE BIG SHINY "BUY NOW" BUTTON?

You could view the legalities and requirements of your website like anything else in business - friend or foe! I encourage you to look again at these as far more than a necessary evil in order to tick a compliance box, but as an opportunity to rapidly build a relationship with visitors to your site. Take advantage of these as opportunities to build that know-like-trust connection with your customers and you will reap the rewards online.

CHAPTER 14

CRACK THE CODE FOR BETTER RESULTS FROM YOUR WEBSITE

IS WAITING FOR YOUR WEBSITE TO LOAD LIKE WAITING FOR PAINT TO DRY?

Not super exciting for you, but you're used to it and some days it's not too bad…

Now imagine what it's like for your customers - or rather, DON'T! Because by the time you've realised how off-putting a slow loading site can be, they've already left. What you may not realise is how badly that slow loading website is affecting not just your customer experience, but can be really **damaging to your brand**.

In 2017, a study by Google of almost one million websites revealed that over **50% of visitors will leave a site** that takes longer than 3 seconds to load!

I've been running my business over twenty years and we've created thousands of websites that have served millions of people all over the world. Yet I remember when I started out, it was considered marketing gospel that you had a mere **eight seconds** to grab your potential customers' attention - count that out load to yourself and tell me if you'd still be waiting for that website to load? No, because back then eight seconds was pretty quick. Now, it's a <u>lifetime</u> - especially if you're aiming at the mobile market which (let's face it) we all are. A sharp-loading site that's mobile-ready is what you want to aim for but remember; this is all about your customer's experience on your website. Get that wrong, for any reason, and they're gone.

IT'S NOT ABOUT SIMPLIFYING YOUR DESIGN EITHER - THE SECRET IS ALL IN THE CODE

The problem is nothing to do with that fabulous design you have had created. It's not because you have too many products on one page, or you've added that embedded feed from your social media channels. It's not even that you've written too much copy! I can tell you one thing I know, above all else; when it comes to web design, it can look as elegant, complex or fancy as you please - if the code behind the site is messy and badly put-together, that page will <u>not</u> load quickly. And your customers are not going to wait.

WHAT'S WORSE, THIS COULD SERIOUSLY IMPACT ON YOUR POSITION IN GOOGLE.

If people regularly click through to your site, then click out again, you earn yourself a high "bounce rate" in Google's eyes - and that means they could label yours as a site people don't find interesting or relevant, leading them to let you slip down the listings.

So, when you're testing your site, or when hiring a new website developer, always ask about your page load speed, and by that I don't just mean your homepage - I mean your whole site. Start with the basics: have the images been optimized? If you have a content management system to make further changes to the site yourself - how will the site handle larger images you upload later? Has this all been coded in to your new website?

We took on a site last year for an incredible training company who taught Sales and Customer Service skills at the highest level. Specialising in Banks and Financial Services companies, their target audience were very much time-poor and wanted great results quickly – but our client's existing website was *painfully* slow to load and had a crazy high bounce rate (over 70%) as a result. Yet, they were happy with the way it looked and the information was all up to date, so we were commissioned to tidy it all up and optimise the code to be faster loading <u>and</u> to load the key information before everything else. The result was astonishing. Within 90 days the bounce rate was below 20% and traffic to the site had *tripled.*

It may sound odd coming from a design agency but, when you're testing your website, don't just look at the design. Think about what's behind it and don't be afraid to ask how that will ultimately help you to rank well in search engines, has it been optimised for page speed, how will it load on mobile? This testing is a key part of our unique, tried and tested five step process; our Website Mastery Method for website success, because we know the importance of this. Not only to please the gods of Google (!) but to deliver a <u>great user experience</u> to your customer - happy customers stay longer and are more likely to make a purchase.

In the meantime, don't get caught up in the code, but don't wait for the page to load ;-)

CHAPTER 15

THE TRUTH, THE WHOLE TRUTH AND NOTHING BUT THE TRUTH...

WHEN IT COMES TO AN OPINION, MOST PEOPLE ARE HAPPY TO SHARE THEIRS - SOMETIMES WHETHER YOU LIKE IT OR NOT!

When it comes to your website however, you really want the *honest* opinions - and that may not be your friends and family.

It's a bit like selling a house. Time and again we hear property experts and popular television shows telling us the decor is not about *your* tastes but those of the potential buyer, who needs to be able to picture *themselves* living there in order to secure the sale.

It's the same with your website - so you need the opinion of others who can view it objectively.

Hopefully by this point you understand the importance of always having your target audience front of mind throughout your website build (revisit Chapter 10 for a walkthrough on this subject), but it's easy to be led astray when you come across a great animation or effect on another website and take a fancy to including it on your own, totally forgetting the preferences and tastes of your target market. So how do we avoid these pitfalls?

ASK YOURSELF, WHO DO I TRUST TO TELL ME THE TRUTH?

Over the years I've heard many people tell me, with great enthusiasm, "my friends and family love it!" And I'm sure that's what they told you. It may even be true - but ask yourself this...

ARE YOUR FRIENDS AND FAMILY YOUR TARGET AUDIENCE?

Do they *truly* represent the majority or bulk of the group you know will actually be looking for your product or service? Are they in the right industry? Would they invest the amount you charge to have their (very real) problem solved? Most importantly, would they tell you the ACTUAL truth if they didn't like what you've created, no matter what the cost to your relationship with them?

If the answer to ALL of these questions is YES - terrific, ask away! You'll get some valuable insight and perhaps some additional features which could really serve your audience. If the answer is NO, you could very well end up with a site your relatives all love - but nobody *buys from* and the time and money you've invested is wasted.

You should always seek these opinions at the early first or second draft stage of your website build in case many changes are needed - to save time and cost further down the line.

So here are a few ideas we've seen work as a far better barometer of your future success, when looking for others - outside your business - to review your website:

1. **Stakeholders.** People who have a vested interest in your *commercial* success, such as shareholders, trustees, non-executive directors - you can even ask your accountant, who may have seen others succeed in similar ventures and can spot any glaring errors

2. **Trusted Clients.** This should be a VERY small pool of those clients who've been with you a good while, who know and share your Company values (revisit Chapter 1 if you need a refresher on identifying and promoting these) and whose opinion really matters to you. These are the sort of clients you want a whole business filled with, so it makes sense to create your new website to appeal to their tastes

3. **Key Staff.** Not everyone in your organisation may understand the concept of your target audience / being selective in this so this is one I wouldn't open up to the whole team - just

the key people who know your customers and their needs on a first-name basis. They're the ones with insights to share and who hear "I can't find it on your website..." more than others might

4. **Your web designer.** Dare we say it, but the person you know who has seen more websites succeed and fail (assuming you chose someone experienced), is the best person to help you learn from others' mistakes. Be prepared to listen to what they say and go with it - even if just for a short period - and trust in your own judgement in choosing to work with them.

We once worked with a terrific company who sold mid-upper-range accessories for a predominantly female market, but the client was obsessed with bargains. Their target audience however were young, affluent and instagram-obsessed - all they wanted was to be seen with the latest bag - not a *bargain*, they wanted status symbols. We stripped away all the "SALE SALE SALE" banners and "Bargain Basement" section, replacing them with high quality, aspirational images and behind-the-scenes glimpses into the handmade and unique nature of the product - values they themselves held dear. Sales through the site quadrupled.

You didn't start your website to create something you want for yourself, you set out to solve someone else's need.

They are the people to ask what they think of your website - *before* it launches - and leave your Mum and Dad to pat you on the back afterwards.

CHECKPOINT: STAGE 3

WE'VE NOW COVERED THE FIVE CRITICAL STEPS OF STAGE 3: CREATION - HOW WAS THAT?

This may be a little "code-y" for some people – no judgement, I'm not a coder myself, all about the pretty pictures! The important thing to remember is this is all WHAT you need to consider / include / decide, and WHY it matters and will contribute to your website's future impact on your business. The HOW to make this reality through code, programming, etc, is what Web

Developers do – find a great one and give them your WHAT and WHY, then leave them to it!

Here is a recap / checklist of the key elements from this stage, in case you need to revisit these:

- **Your website text:**
  - Why this should always speak directly to your dream client profile, focusing on the features and benefits to showcase the result of working with / buying from you, are you a "we" or a "they" and why this matters
- **Image is everything:**
  - Pros and cons of choosing stock images versus your own, showing the detail and the big picture, are you faces or places, focus on solutions not problems
- **Legal Requirements:**
  - Assurances around privacy, understanding the importance of cookies, what are the essentials for your local laws
- **Code:**
  - Including the optimum keywords and phrases, tying key words to your page content, do you need plugins, page load speed and the latest displays

- Don't skimp on revisions:
  - o Sharing your creation with others, involving the right people with insight over input, finding a trusted source, being prepared to revisit – or even start over!

Does everything in this list look familiar? If so, great! You can move on to the next section safe in the knowledge that you have enough information to create a framework and content, on your own or with a trusted supplier. If not, jump back now and review the chapters in this Stage to work through the exercise in each one.

Remember you don't have to do this alone – or learn a single string of code, you don't have time! Use your understanding to gather quotes from people you'd like to work with – if that's us, reach out and book a quick session with me at www.websitemasterybook.com today.

STAGE 4

LAUNCH

CHAPTER 16

CATCH YOUR CLIENTS ON THE MOVE

THERE'S A GREAT EXPRESSION IN MARKETING-SPEAK; MEET YOUR CLIENTS WHERE THEY ARE NOW.

For your business, that means delivering just as great a user experience at the bus stop as the desktop...

The fact is, we're all more attached to our phones and tablets than ever, and your potential clients are no different. Latest stats show that over 80% of internet users are actively accessing the web every day from a mobile device - and every one of them expects a seamless and enjoyable experience on your site, regardless of whether they're on an iPhone, Android tablet or laptop!

So, we know your potential customers *expect* a great user experience on the go, but how *important* is it where it really matters - your bottom line? Improving your conversion rate from "visitor" to "customer" is my mission in life and there are many factors to consider - see Chapter 11 for more tips and advice on this topic - but is it *really* worth the extra time and effort?

IN A WORD - YES!

Not only is a great mobile site nice to look at, meeting your customers' needs in this way has them feeling seen, heard and (critically) *understood* by your company and that builds rapport - fast! It's not enough to sell the widget or service they're looking for, your clients really do care WHO they're dealing with and if they decide you've "obviously not bothered" with addressing their needs at this base level, they'll walk.

Good news is you can avoid this scenario with a healthy portion of testing (see Chapter 19 on the importance of testing your website) and really dig into the Responsiveness of your website before it's even launched.

Responsive testing is, put simply, looking at your site on multiple devices, platforms and browsers. Do the buttons work or are they too small for fingers on a smartphone touch screen? Does it look as good for Apple desktop users as for PC - and which should you prioritise for your target audience – revisit Chapter 10 on defining your target client persona if you need help with this.

Then there's orientation, and how you address this comes down to the nature of your website. If you're delivering online video content, mobiles viewers will most likely hold their phone in a sideways / landscape position to view this - does the rest of the page still work and make sense if they then scroll on beyond the video?

NAVIGATION MENUS ARE ANOTHER POTHOLE TO AVOID ON THIS JOURNEY TOO.

Most laptop and smartphone website displays favour the "Burger Menu" - the three horizontal lines at the top of the page which drop down on touch to display all the pages. For a while there was a trend to apply these to desktop views too, but in the main, website visitors like a full menu on a desktop. Again, if you have sub menus and subpages on your menu - will the burger format support this or does your website need to deliver navigation to mobile users in a completely different way?

As ever, it all comes down to: who is your target audience?

Take the charity we recently worked with who were targeting older people in their homes and hoping to engage with them to garner their opinions and input on a new range of community services. Quite rightly, the project management team identified from the outset that their users were less likely to be accessing the site on a smartphone, but what else should they be thinking about? Working with them on this, we clarified that their customer base was probably also using older monitors (typically smaller than the smart modern ones they planned to test on) and also likely older browsers as many were wary of upgrades being downloaded. We coded their site to automatically detect the user's platform (PC or Mac), browser and screen size, then deliver a positive, easy-to-navigate experience for them based entirely on their personal situation.

RESPONSES AND ENGAGEMENT INCREASED DRAMATICALLY!

There are so many technical aspects to think about when creating your website but, if you really want to see great results, never forget it's not about the tech - it's about the human being using it. Give them an intuitive, easy experience and they'll be loyal to you, with no clicking away as the bus pulls up...

CHAPTER 17

WHY YOU NEED THE HOST WITH THE MOST

While you're busy running your business each day, if you're anything like me, you probably don't give your own website a second thought. I mean, why would you?

IT'S JUST THERE, ISN'T IT? OR IS IT...?

The difference between your website's success and failure is based on a multitude of factors (*see previous Chapters for just a few to consider*), but there's one key essential which cannot be underrated - **rock solid hosting**. Without that in place, the dreaded words "This web page is not available" flash before your potential customers' eyes and, shortly afterwards, they're gone.

I recently read that 88% of online consumers will not return to a site after a bad experience like a failure to load, slow loading or a security warning - all of which are massively dependent on the hosting account the website sits in.

For the non-techies among us; your hosting account is simply the space on the internet your website sits in. Sometimes this also gives your email a place to live, but for this Chapter we're focussing on the website only ;-)

Now picture this; instead of the dreaded Page Not Found message, your customers see your site in all its glory, quickly loaded onto their screen and with that magical padlock at the top of the page so they're completely <u>confident</u> to enter their personal or purchasing details, safe in the knowledge that this will be well taken care of. How much more likely do you imagine they'll be to connect with you and become another satisfied customer?

SO, LET'S CRACK THIS, HERE'S EXACTLY WHAT YOU NEED TO CONSIDER WHEN CHOOSING YOUR WEBSITE HOST:

1. **Shared server versus dedicated server.** Put simply, this is the difference between your website having its own private suite with all bells and whistles, additional security, etc - versus a Shared Server where you're bunking in with everyone else on the block. Most clients prefer the sound of Dedicated space, but it comes at a cost and may not be necessary for your website's needs - always speak with your web developer if you're not sure on this one.

2. **What's included?** Here at FAT, we favour Outlook 365 for our email as it works nicely across all our devices - PC and Mac - and makes it easy for us to filter messages directly to the right member of the team. You may prefer your email to come into your host server so you can access it through webmail from anywhere so you need to know if your host supports that. Similarly, visitor statistics reports are included as standard on

our hosting packages so you have unrestricted access to see who's looked at your site, how long they stayed, which pages they viewed, which search engine they used to find you and what they typed in to get there, etc. If this is important to you, you'll want this as part of your hosting as that's where it all happens.

3. **Show me the padlock.** With most anti-virus packages now helpfully displaying warnings if a site doesn't have security built in beside your listing in the search results, that's an easy way to lower your click rate, so be sure to ask for SSL with your website hosting account. This displays the nice padlock we mentioned earlier and all of the endearing qualities that offers to your potential clients once they're on your site. Above all else, it's a mark of trust and as we know, that's the first step to converting a visitor to a paying customer.

4. **We need backup!** Technically, yes you can download a copy of your own website every night and pop this as a backup onto a disk somewhere safe, but is that the best use of your time? Far better to choose a hosting

account with automated, nightly backups - so they're not happening during the day and potentially slowing your site down for active visitors - and keeping copies of these for a few weeks JUST in case you need to roll back to a previous date for any reason. This is not one you want to learn the hard way!

Having run my company for over twenty years now, I've lost count of how many approaches I've had from hosting companies vying for our business and promising rock-solid hosting on their super-reliable servers. Taking the time to fully review all of the points above - plus asking about things like monitoring, alerts and support if anything goes wrong, where the data is physically stored - has shown me that you really do get what you pay for. We now host all of our sites with Amazon Web Services as they offer all of the above and more - but that does mean we're not the cheapest hosting offering around.

One client raised this very point with me when we built their ecommerce site a few years ago, in fact they were quite vocal on the subject of the "far cheaper" hosting offering they'd found elsewhere. As one of our core values is to always Start in Service, we were happy to install their newly completed website onto their preferred host server with another provider, just as they requested.

TWO WEEKS LATER THEY WERE BACK

Turned out that in that short time they had received multiple reports of the website being unavailable when customers were trying to buy. That was bad enough, but after a late-night attempt to "just quickly change something on the website", the customer had accidentally deleted a whole chunk of their site by mistake - only to find there was no backup. That's a feeling nobody wants and, now they're <u>safely</u> hosted with us, they should never experience again.

The key to choosing the right host for your website is to learn which questions to ask - then don't be afraid to ask them! Your web developer should be your first port of call but, if they can't help, reach out and let's talk about getting your website on a stable footing. Giving you one less thing to think about!

CHAPTER 18

READY FOR LIFT-OFF!

IT DOESN'T MATTER HOW LONG YOU'VE SPENT PERFECTING YOUR NEW WEBSITE...

Get the launch process wrong and you could drop off the map altogether.

You see, launching a brand-new website can be challenge enough, but *replacing* an old site requires a whole different set of checklists and tick boxes to make sure *everything* has been covered because, if not, you're in real danger of losing that valuable online presence <u>and</u> reputation you've spent so long creating.

Think of it like moving house. Just think of all the excitement of choosing your new home, new furniture / décor, meeting the new neighbours, checking out local amenities – it's all great, positive stuff, right? So, it's easy to get caught up in that and overlook the essentials which will make your move go smoothly – that also applies to moving from your old website to the bright, shiny new one you're about to launch.

We're talking about all of the nitty gritty essentials you need to consider when moving home; such as booking the moving van, packing your stuff, redirecting your mail, telling all your friends where to find you, inviting them to the house warming party – the list goes on.

In website terms, these are all things you need to consider too. At the basic level, carefully choosing the date to launch your new site is critical; moving it outside business hours may seem like a good plan, but will your new hosting company or tech support team be available to help you at 4pm on a Sunday if something doesn't go to plan?

Then there's all of that great content on your old website, which your previous online visitors may have bookmarked to revisit later – what will happen to those links if they click them after your website has moved?

This applies to search engines too, as they won't instantly update all of their links to pages you have listed in search results, no matter how nicely you ask! It takes time, and a little bit of tech 😊

THE SECRET IS IN THE CHECKLISTS.

As a process-driven company, we pretty much have a checklist for everything – and we've not regretted a single one. You see, checklists give you a blueprint, a really clear map to follow so you don't get lost or miss any vital steps - so the move is effortless.

I recall one client who'd been with us for a few years but was woo-ed away by a slick salesperson promising champagne results on a beer-bottle budget! The dream they sold looked good, promises were made, and the site was "moved" away to its new online home.

Except it wasn't a "move" at all – it was the equivalent of burning the house down!

Integrations with third-party suppliers that had worked for years stopped working. Visitor data and statistics were wiped, emails disappeared, content was missing in action and Google couldn't find them for love nor money.

When the call came, we knew we had to act quickly to recover all the lost data, images and content, and start work straight away to undo the damage done to the all-important search engine listings. We put a plan in place to recover and rebuild, using our own checklist as the "packing list" showing us what needed to be where, then making that happen – much to the client's relief!

If you're in the throes of creating or restructuring your existing website, the thing to remember is take the time to plan carefully. Just like those packing boxes; if everything you need to take with you is clearly labelled and carefully stored, the move will go smoothly and you'll be sitting pretty in your new (online) home in no time. Now, where did I put the kettle…?

CHAPTER 19

YOU THINK IT'S ALL OVER...

5 ESSENTIAL CHECKS TO MAKE <u>BEFORE</u> YOU ANNOUNCE YOUR NEW WEBSITE TO THE WORLD

Congratulations! You've *finally* finished and launched your new website - doesn't that feel great?

All those months of poring over the content, choosing all the best images, creating that lead-magnet and preparing your mailing list for all those new orders coming in - all brought you to this point in time and WOW are you ready to stop now!

IF YOU DO, IT'S ALL OVER

Scary, but true - because if there's one thing I've learned in over two decades spent creating award winning websites and ecommerce systems, it is this: the *final* step is the most dangerous for the future success of your website. Stumble now (or skip this last stage) and it will all have been for nought.

SO, HERE'S THE GOOD NEWS: THAT NEEDN'T BE THE CASE!

Listen, I get it. All that hard work that you've put into your site (whether you built it yourself or had an agency do this for you, you still had to put in the work), *will* pay off if you've included all the essentials at each stage of development - we just need to cross the final few hurdles to avoid these well-known pitfalls before you announce your new baby to the world and start tweeting your new web address for all the world to see.

Here are the last five things to check-off your quality assurance checklist after your new website is finished but before you start the PR machine rolling:

You think it's all over...

1. **Backup your previous site.** "But I don't need it any more" you cry. Well, hopefully that is the case - but what if some of your lovely existing content didn't copy across to the new site correctly and you need to "just pop back into the old site and grab a copy" - only you can't? Taking a backup of your old site is a simple step with massive potential impact.

2. **Just one more test.** Of course you've already tested every email and enquiry link on your new website (if you've read anything else in this book before this point, I would hope so!), but *just one more* quick test on your newly launched site is always worth it. If you have a team, you can make this a bit of fun too - offer a prize to the first person to find a broken link! Better that Annie in Accounts discovers your enquiry form goes to an email account you no longer use, than your next potential (and now lost) customer?

3. **Buy now - or pay later.** Another test - your online payment or purchase mechanism, or Buy Now button as it's known to most humans! You may have tested this repeatedly

during the development phase but the live site is a different environment and you *need* to know that when your customers start landing on your shiny new website, filled with excitement and the urge to purchase from you, they can do exactly that.

4. **Where am I?** All sites benefit from an online sitemap, which helps the search engines find what you do and where to send people looking for those goods or services you provide so well. During development stage these can include links to temporary pages or web addresses - make sure you check these are nowhere to be seen after launch.

5. **Formerly known as....?** If a new domain name was part of your new website, make sure after launch that any old or previous domain names have been correctly redirected to your new site to save you that mortifying Page Not Found message when hordes of new customers head to your new site.

The latter point is one that still trips people up today. Back in the early days of internet, unscrupulous "developers" would register domains in their own name, meaning unhappy customers who moved on were forced to buy new domain after new domain with each new website incarnation. We helped one client track down FIVE previously-used varieties of their domain name and properly redirected these to the new website we created - and the visitor numbers to the new site SHOT up! Seems that previous customers of theirs had been searching for them for years and some even thought they were no longer in business - *eek!* Had we not run through these checks as part of our own quality assurance, they could have lost vital business at this critical point.

You've done a great job on your website yes, but there's *always* room for improvement - and if you apply it just before you announce your latest creation to the world - even if you *don't* find any errors - I guarantee you'll be glad you did.

CHAPTER 20

IF YOU BUILD IT, WILL THEY FIND IT?

IF YOU CREATE A WEBSITE AND NOBODY CAN SEE IT, DOES IT REALLY EXIST AT ALL...?

You may not be a technically-minded person, you may not even LIKE tech very much, but you accept that having a website *is* necessary for your Company. You worked hard to overcome your fears and perhaps preconceptions about what it would take to create a site and now it's done (and you quite like it) — where are the droves of new enquiries you thought would come flooding in?

CAN'T THEY SEE THE EFFORT YOU'VE PUT IN HERE???

Truth is, new websites don't even appear in Google results for up to FOUR WEEKS, and even then, those who *do* appear may be several pages down the listings before they begin the long slog to the top of the pile. So, what can you do about it?

There are several tricks, tips and myths about the dark art of Search Engine Optimisation you may have heard, but the first thing I want you to know is this: it WILL take time. Unless you pay a blank cheque to Google to instantly appear at the top (in which case you need to be sure you're not paying to be found for your company name, but that's a whole other book), a brand-new site could take weeks to appear at all — and even then it's not guaranteed. On the plus side; achieving a good listing in Google will make a difference to the traffic your website sees, and traffic is the first step on the path to more enquires, more conversion and more customers.

With little or no listing though, your site just doesn't exist in the public eye - or in their mind - and that could spell disaster for your company.

SO, WHAT DOES IT TAKE TO BE VISIBLE, AND IS THAT ENOUGH TO ACHIEVE YOUR WEBSITE GOALS?

The first step is to have specific goals in mind for your website in the first instance, as without them you simply cannot measure its success — or the return on your investment. Goals for your website could include some or all of the following:

- Increased awareness of your company or brand in a specific geographic region
- Your site appearing on page one of the results for one specific key phrase (you can build on this later by adding more of course, but start with an achievable goal)
- This one is key (as this is how you'll measure the effectiveness of those above): new customer enquiries received via the website each week.

Take five minutes to sit down with your chosen web design company *before* they begin any work on your new website and agree with them what you want the site to achieve and how you'll measure this. This exercise helps you both to better understand the aims of the project and all reach a result you're happy with. Remember to make these measurable though; "more enquiries" could mean 2 a week instead of 1 - will that be enough for you?

Then work with your deign agency to identify the best keywords and phrases you'd like the site to be found for. Contrary to some misconceptions, this is not your designer's job as you know best which key words and phrases you hear from your clients and customers, and only you know when you'd like your site to pop up. It's your designer / developer's job to then code these words and phrases into your site effectively to ensure that happens.

Ask your agency to look into the most / least popular searches on Google for your industry or profession: you may be surprised to find that what you think people are typing in to find companies like yours and what they actually are, is very different.

WAIT! YOU'VE ALREADY BUILT YOUR SITE AND NOW ITS TOO LATE TO IMPLEMENT ANY OF THIS STUFF?

Nope, this can all be carried out retrospectively. Though it may require a bit of unpicking of what you already have, don't worry if you've passed the "brand new site" stage - there is still hope!

Like the company we met recently who were nearing the end of their first year of trading in a very specialist field, with little (if any) competition in their local region — yet they'd received NOT ONE single enquiry through their new website in <u>over nine months</u>. Needless to say, the owner was feeling a little less than thrilled with the results achieved by his previous website supplier and thought perhaps there just wasn't the call for his professional services in the area. He'd reached the point where he actually thought his business was a "non-starter".

We looked into local searches for his service and found that people WERE looking, but his site didn't appear at all — probably leaving them as frustrated as he was, as they couldn't find a local expert. Having identified what this massive potential audience was searching for, we then took over the management of his site and optimised it for these key search terms and phrases, then added clear calls to action throughout the site to further encourage these newly-found website visitors to reach out to him. Yet for all this work and effort, the site itself looked the same to the human eye as we hadn't changed the design or layout (other than a few buttons here and there) — it was all code magic behind the scenes.

The new website was launched on a Friday and we requested Google "re-index" it to refresh its opinion (for want of a better term!) as to what the website was all about. The following Monday morning we received a call from this VERY happy client to say he'd had his *first ever* enquiry through the website and had already spoken with the potential new client — who turned out to be a large local authority and exactly the sort of work he was looking for!

So if your website is not performing the way you would like it to, start by asking yourself what that actually looks like. Map out just a few key aims — and how you'll measure these — and make these as much a part of the build process as choosing the colour you like!

If your website arrives on the scene optimised and ready to be easily found in search results and listings, your audience may be just a click away.

CHECKPOINT: STAGE 4

ALMOST THERE! PREPARING TO LAUNCH (STAGE 4) COMPLETE!

Such an important stage, as skipping parts of this after all your hard work could send you off with a fizzle, not a bang! Personally, I've always found some people are just *wired* for the level of detail and fact-checking this stage demands in order to get the right result. If that's not your area of expertise, pull in a member of your team or trusted supplier and make sure those T's are crossed and I's are dotted!

Let's recap some of the key elements mentioned in this stage, in case you need to revisit any of the exercises around these:

- Is it responsive:
  - Does it look just as good on Mac or PC, is it fast on desktop and mobile (what if you hold the phone sideways?), are the menus fine on touch screens

- Hosting your site:
  - Navigating shared versus a dedicated server, does this include visitor statistics, is your email service included, what about security and backups

- Before launch:
  - Ensure the website correctly displays social links, transferring your existing Google Analytics account, taking backups from your old host, redirecting links to pages of your previous site

- On Launch:
  - Take a backup of your previous site, test online payments work correctly, double check purchase and enquiry systems, create a technical sitemap file for visibility, don't lose your previous domain

- **Will they find it:**
  - Specify which regions you want to be found in, choose on specific phrase and build on that, measure your return on investment.

I'll grant you; this stage IS a bit techy – but you don't have to be! Surround yourself with good, knowledgeable people who have experience and your additional knowledge of what you've learned here will make you a formidable team. Refresh your memory on these by revisiting the chapters in this Stage to work through the exercise in each one.

Does your web designer have technical server management experience? If not, you could come unstuck! Always ask about this aspect of the build before you decide on who will build your site. If you want to see what that looks like, reach out and book a quick session with me at www.websitemasterybook.com and I'll unravel the jargon.

STAGE 5

SUPPORT

CHAPTER 21

WHO IS WATCHING YOUR WEBSITE?

WHEN IT COMES TO YOUR WEBSITE, AS BUSINESS OWNERS IT IS EASY TO GET *(*AHEM*)* CARRIED AWAY SOMETIMES OBSESSING ABOUT HOW MANY VISITORS YOUR SITE GETS, HOW LONG THEY STAY, ETC.

No judgement! We all go through phases of this at some point but I'm not talking about *visitors* watching your website, I'm asking who is watching your site FOR you?

"My site works fine; it doesn't need watching" is something I hear all too often but - be honest here - when did you last *really* check your own website?

THOROUGHLY? And if you looked at 7pm on a Friday night and your site was DOWN, would you even know where to begin?

Scary fact, but according to the website Small Biz Trends, latest research suggests that the average website is down three hours a month due to the downtime of web host providers. Given there are over 1.6 billion websites currently out there (according to recent figures), your chances of this happening to you are teeny tiny, particularly with a stable, reputable hosting company taking care of your site (read Chapter 17 on Choosing a Host with the Most) but finding yourself in that small percentage with no idea just how long your website has been like that can make any business owner's blood run cold.

SO, WHAT CAN YOU DO TO PROTECT YOURSELF FROM THIS SCENARIO?

The good news is there are many ways to automatically monitor your site's uptime or availability at little or no cost, so at least you'll be aware if there IS a problem - long before your customers let you know! What you may not realise is the many incredible insights and advantages to be gained in consistent, structured monitoring of your website activity - and how to use that to measure the effectiveness of your marketing elsewhere.

Take your standard website statistics for example. To the trained eye, this is a veritable treasure trove of invaluable information and far more than a passing glance at how popular your website is this week! Is all the hard work you've put in to marketing your Company on LinkedIn recently paying off in clicks through to your website? And what are they doing when they get there?

For example, large visitor numbers to your online enquiry form may first appear to be a positive thing but, upon checking the inbox for these enquiries in your office, they don't appear to have come through? Could it be your form demands more personal information than someone is prepared to give on first contact (good to know, so you can simplify this), or there could be a technical issue with the delivery - when did you last test your own enquiry form?

That's just one of a group of simple, manageable tasks you should be carrying out on your site on a regular, scheduled, consistent basis - ideally once a month as a minimum - check out my Website Insight series on our YouTube Channel for the top issues to watch out for:

www.youtube.com/@fatpromotions

ANOTHER IS TO WATCH FOR ANY SUDDEN PEAKS OR TROUGHS IN YOUR OVERALL SITE VISITOR NUMBERS.

One client of ours runs a hugely successful membership website in the Southern Hemisphere and was delighted to see their website visitor numbers start to rapidly climb over the course of 24 hours. Thankfully, the monitoring we have in place as part of their ongoing Support Package had already spotted the trend and alerted our team. As the numbers continued to climb, we quickly identified the "visitors" were actually automated bots from an overseas address and were attempting to maliciously overload the site and bring it down. Our team took swift action and any potential disaster was thankfully averted without any negative impact on the live website.

Watching your own website may not be your idea of fun, but it will be someone else's. Make arrangements now to find someone who will do this for you and you can enjoy your Friday evenings in peace, knowing your site is out there safe and stable, serving your ideal clients day and night.

CHAPTER 22

LAST UPDATED...

"WE ONLY HAD OUR WEBSITE REBUILT SIX MONTHS AGO!"

I often hear business owners say this - without realising that usually means the content on your site is already six months old. Would you read a newspaper from six months ago?

Research from User Experience experts at Microsoft crunched the numbers to analyse over 205,000 different web pages and over 10,000 visits - and discovered you have a mere **TEN SECONDS** in which visitors to your website will decide whether they want to engage with you or not. If they've been to your site before and see nothing new to grab their attention, chances are they're about to click away and you lose a potential customer who'll never know about that amazing new product you just launched, or read that glowing testimonial about a recently completed project.

The search engines (and there are more than one!) LOVE a regularly updated website - it makes them look good to be delivering the latest, up-to-date results in their listings. They are more likely to favour your company in results above similar - but way older - content from similar sites. **Give them what they want and you reap the benefit of better ranking and more traffic.** Leave your site to wither under old or outdated information (how many times have you heard "oh, they don't work here anymore, they shouldn't be on the website"?) and you risk dropping not only in the search results, but out of favour altogether with those potential clients who do reach your site. They rarely return later to see if things have changed...

Regularly updating with great content relevant to your right-fit client can yield other rewards you may not have considered too. In over two decades of working with established UK Companies with plans to expand their online reach and impact, we have seen countless occasions when a programme of continuous improvement had significant *internal* benefits within your own team. This could be the star player who steps up to take on responsibility for new content or checking over what your site already says and reflecting any changes to that - they have a new role with visibility and impact - who springs to mind on your team who would *love* to take that on?

Avoid a costly mistake here by clearly defining what the role entails then <u>asking</u> who in your team would like to take this on. This is rarely a role you can "pick" someone for without their buy-in, having this done badly can be as damaging as not doing it at all.

So you can see the perks and prominence of regular website updates, you've defined the role and (hopefully) found a willing volunteer to make it happen - how to get started?

Here are three steps to get the ball rolling and set you on the road to effortless, regular updates:

1. **That which is scheduled is done.** The person responsible for your updates (even if it has to be you to begin with), MUST schedule at least a one-hour slot each month in their calendar for this. Same time, same day, once a month and nothing is permitted to move it - no meetings, no "just need to finish this first" - set it in stone and leave it alone!

2. **Start small.** Setting yourself the task to write a new case study, update your portfolio, change all your photos in the gallery and create a new blog post every month is a full-time job, and not a very fun one. Aim to review and update ONE page a month is enough - and probably more than you're doing already. Small steps are still steps in the right direction, aim for constant improvement, not inventing the wheel every four weeks.

3. **Plan ahead.** You have the time set aside, you have a manageable task to do within that time, don't waste the first 15 minutes wondering what to do with it. Spend a rainy January afternoon writing a simple bullet list

of possible tasks you can refer back to - such as topics to write blogs about, pages of your site to review and work through, new products not yet shown online, etc. Then choose one of these each month and focus your hour on that. Easy.

We went through this process with one of our clients, an established and successful insurance company who weren't sure what they could do to increase their visibility and online engagement. They held a strategy session with us at the beginning of the year to plan ahead just as laid out above and, within an hour, they had a full year's updates and marketing topics planned out. **We then watched as their visitor numbers and enquires grew month on month that year - no coincidence!**

You wouldn't continue to have the same conversation with someone over and over in your life - so why expect your clients to do that in your business? Keep your website updated and your content fresh - while making it fun and easy for your team - and you *will* see the difference in how engaged people are both within and outside your office walls.

CHAPTER 23

READ ME FIRST

NOBODY EVER READS THE INSTRUCTIONS

Okay, maybe *some* people do (like me!) but, in over two decades spent creating custom-made websites and software systems, I can count on three fingers how many clients read the instructions for their shiny new site.

And that's okay when you have someone on hand to help when you later want to change or fix something. Which you will... as your website is an evolving thing and needs love and attention on an ongoing basis. We're talking post-launch support and how to plan ahead for anything you - or your customers - may need.

You see, it's not just the little tweaks and changes *you* would like to make going forward. Users / members / shoppers on your website may also need a helping hand from time to time. Plan for this - and have systems in place in advance - and not only will your customers have a positive experience on your website, but you won't be bothered by requests for forgotten passwords or reminders to login interrupting your time or your team throughout the day.

That means time better spent on planning your next product or service improvement to take your business or charity forward and reach more of the people you want to work with.

And let's be honest - how often are you *really* going to bother updating your website if each time you do, you have to call someone else and ask for "a quick reminder" on how to login and make a simple change?

SO WHERE AND WHEN DO YOU START?

The latter is easy - before your website launches, make sure you have a written copy (or even better, video instructions) of how your website content management system works - and try this out for yourself. Ask your developer for a hidden test page that only you can see, when you / your team can have a play without fear of displaying any errors to your waiting public. This gives the less-technically-minded a safe space to practice and overcome any reservations around making changes, so they're ready to help when you need it.

For your customers; review your new site as they would - or ask someone who's not yet seen your website to do so and document their experience for you. Simple interactions they have on your site which may seem perfectly obvious to you or your developer, but does it make sense to the public? Start with a list of these points in your website where the customer has to interact and anticipate any queries they may have, such as:

- Where to login to their account (is the button to this *blatantly* obvious?)
- Entering their password (is there an automated reminder system)
- Frequently asked questions (could an online Help Bot answer these and save your team precious time?)

A site we created for a national chain of care homes makes great use of this feature on their site, with an automated Help Bot addressing simple queries on a daily basis. This has been extended to support not only existing customers in need of reminders for logins and enquiries, but also answering those regularly-asked initial queries from potential new customers - reducing demands on staff time and moving them further along the customer journey without any effort.

Work your way through the list you come up with (remembering you can always add to this later as your experience of using the site grows) and **plan ahead for huge success with little effort.**

CHAPTER 24

3 KILLER SIGNS YOUR WEBSITE IS OUTDATED

...AND JUST HOW BADLY THAT CAN DAMAGE YOUR BUSINESS.

Hurray! Your new website is done and live, so now you can sit back and relax - just waiting for the results to roll in, right? Wrong! Truth is, the hard work is just beginning, and that is keeping your website current, engaging and running smoothly - all things that require attention on an ongoing basis.

Truth is, if people are looking for your products or services, the first place they look is online. This is great news! This means your website has the opportunity to WOW them (if it can be found, see Chapter 20 for tips on this), as well as build credibility and reputation to lovingly nudge them over the line into becoming a client of yours. Where many sites fall down is; the attention span of people looking online is shorter than ever and if they arrive at your site to find that the information on there is out of date / hasn't changed in months - or worse still, parts of the site aren't even working (*shocked face*) - they're not going to stick around.

But hey, you don't have TIME to be constantly checking or updating your site - you have a business to run! Besides, (you tell yourself) it's not that bad, nobody will *really* know if the information is out of date ...will they?

To help you properly assess if it's time you found some support for your site, let's identify three easy things to look for in *your* website today, to tell you if it's time you had some help with this:

DOES IT LOOK GREAT ON YOUR (NEW) MOBILE PHONE?

With new models being launched almost daily, it is hard to keep up with the demands of smaller / larger screens, high resolution / fast loading options for your website on every brand of mobile phone. But if you don't have this regularly checked, you'll be effectively alienating a huge swathe of early adopters - people who can't wait to grab the latest technology to improve their lives. If your target audience includes young professionals, this is a particular concern for your site. A regular check will ensure your site stays up to date with the tech in their pocket and you stay in their mind as a company who moves with the times.

HAS THE TECHNOLOGY MOVED ON?

I'm no fan of change for the change's sake, so we're not talking about redesigning your site every six months because orange is so "in" right now! I'm talking about the nuts-and-bolts technology your website runs on. This can include plug-ins for your content management system - have they had an upgrade lately? If not, there's a potential security hole in your bucket that may leave your website vulnerable to attack or even being hijacked altogether. Another thing to check is Google algorithm updates. When these change, you may need to make changes to your site just to maintain your existing visibility and position in the listings. If you aren't checking these things regularly your site could not only be left behind, but could disappear altogether.

(THIS IS THE REAL KILLER) - DOES YOUR ENQUIRY SYSTEM ACTUALLY *WORK*?

Be honest - when was the last time you <u>actually</u> went to your website and filled out the enquiry form / hit the Call Me Back button / sent yourself a message? Most clients of ours are simply (and understandably) far too busy to do this on a consistent basis, but without it you could be missing vital sales and enquiries. Testing needs to be carried out using an external email address ideally, and again, on a regular basis for true stability and peace of mind.

When I started my company many years ago, almost every client said they would "take care of" this aspect of ongoing care for their new website. I quickly learned that they just didn't have time - and anyway why would they, when websites weren't their area of expertise? That's why we introduced our Maintenance & Support plans, to provide ongoing care and technical guidance for every website we built.

The value of this was really brought home with one client who owned a small chain of hotels in the Cotswolds, each in a stunning setting and an absolute magnet for the wedding market. We created several sites for them, each designed to appeal to this specific target audience and each with an ongoing Maintenance & Support package to provide all of these with consistent, continuous monthly checks of all the key points above, plus carrying out any updates they required as we went. In one round of regular checks, we noticed that although the enquiry form was being submitted, nobody was replying. Further testing showed the enquiries were going to a specific email address at the hotel, which we could see was not being monitored. A quick call to the manager and some re-routing of their internal IT system and they avoided a very near miss of a £20k wedding booking enquiry who was about to go elsewhere as they hadn't heard back!

This is the reason that regular reviews and testing of your website (pubic display and hidden tech / codes bits) is so vital to your ongoing success. Try not to think of it as yet another thing you have to do but something you can schedule as a regular, ongoing check that your website is visible and functional - because that's what really delivers results for your business.

CHAPTER 25

WHERE TO NEXT FOR YOUR WEBSITE?

NEVER MIND WHERE YOU ARE NOW, WHERE YOU *GOING*?

In an ever-changing world, no industry stands still - and nor does the technology they use. How can you harness this potential when you don't know how it applies to you?

Do an internet search for how often companies update their website and you'll see every answer from "monthly" to "several times a day" - but we're not talking about changing the text or images on your newly-completed site. We're talking about a website that <u>takes work off your desk</u>.

We've all heard about automation and how it is the most effective way to reduce production times and manual input - but you're running a service-based business, not a factory full of robots - where do you even begin?

You may hear tales of other businesses and how they've "digitised" their offering, leading to claims of shorter turnaround times and higher profit margins. Yet, looking at your organisation, you may see people doing those repetitive tasks day after day and you can't imagine how a computer is going to run that for you - *and whether that means losing the human touch your Company really values.*

Here's the key thing to remember: automation does NOT mean losing the human touch. Far from it in fact, automation done well can make your team's life easier, as well as your own.

Truth is, none of us know what we don't know. This is where you're going to really benefit from some guidance, but you can still make a start on a list of those repetitive daily tasks which really need addressing:

First step is to get your team on board. Ask them to list the top 3 things they are asked to do more than twice a week. Ask them not to filter this, but to give the 3 which spring immediately to mind. These are your key time eaters to be added to your list and typically these include items such as sending out brochures, sending email attachments, etc.

Next, look at what you ask of your clients. Do they have to submit information to you / sign documents / send copies of paperwork? Moving these *off their desk* and online will save you <u>both</u> time AND showcase your Company as modern and innovative

Finally, review the software you use on a daily basis - are you getting the full potential of this? You'd be amazed how many pieces of tech can talk to each directly without you having to manually upload / import / type-in the details from somewhere else and this can save you exponential amounts of time.

We carried out this exercise with a large client of ours who offer specialist, high-quality asset insurance. As well as wanting their site to appear more modern and engage with a younger audience, they needed to automate many of the manual tasks required in processing their lengthy application forms, especially given that their customers are short of time and need a quick online quote to work from. The new mobile-friendly website we created gave them the visual appeal they wanted along with a practical, high-tech solution to move all those nasty paper-based forms into slick, online versions which slot straight into the client's in-house software at the click of a button – saving their team effort and valuable time every single day.

I often say to clients that although I want their website to look fabulous and represent them authentically online, if it's not earning its place in your business by also taking work off your desk - it should be. Look at the list you've created using the steps above and head into research mode to find out just how many of these daily tasks you don't need a human to do - freeing up your valuable team to do the work they love and never have to hit Copy and Paste again. That's possibly the biggest positive impact your website can have.

CHECKPOINT: STAGE 5

AND WE'RE DONE – STAGE 5: SUPPORT IS COMPLETE – NOW THE REAL WORK BEGINS…!

Your new website is live - hurrah! Take a moment, pat yourself on the back and revel in the positive feedback from clients, contacts and team… then take a breath and start planning the next steps. You see, your site is never finished. It's an organic, living thing which reflects your Company in the best possible light.

Here is your recap / checklist of the key elements mentioned in this stage, to refresh your memory:

- **Monitoring:**
  - Schedule regular site checks and testing, submit new content to search engines, keep a regular eye on visitor statistics to spot peaks and troughs – and identify the causes
- **Always be updating:**
  - As you grow your website must reflect changes in your product or service offering, update team pages at least twice a year (those photos!), post regular news items or blogs - depending on your target audience
- **HELP!!!**
  - Arrange access to Content Management System training or documentation for future use, give customers automated reminders for passwords, create written guides for email settings and accessing visitor stats, have someone you can call when needed
- **Regular reviews:**
  - Run a monthly site check and test enquiry systems, plan ahead for monthly / seasonal / peak times'

updates, review as a team quarterly / annually to ensure still current and relevant

- Looking ahead:
  - Which mundane everyday tasks can you take off your desk and onto your site, automating your scheduling / marketing / payments online, making your website part of your in-house systems.

Think of your website as your best-ever employee; one who can always recite your products and services flawlessly, always shows up to meet new clients looking smart, and one who actively finds ways to take work off your desk and build the business.

Just like that employee, your website needs ongoing training, care and investment to make it happen!

DEDICATE TIME TO THIS AND YOU WILL REAP THE BENEFITS!

Who on your team could manage these regular updates and monitoring for you? Leave this for "somebody" to do and you may find "everybody" thinks it's someone else's job so "nobody" does it 😠

Chat with us about support and update packages to keep your site going and growing – just like your business! Reach out and book a quick session with me at www.websitemasterybook.com and I'll unravel the jargon.

NOW WHAT?

TIME TO GET STARTED!

Ever heard the expression "start with the end in mind?" - well that's where you find yourself now. The book is over but the real fun is just beginning!

I've given you the full and unabridged step-by-step guide to each and every essential element and ingredient I have seen elevate businesses (and organisations) *exponentially* through digital transformation. On our journey together through these pages, we have discovered the (sometimes horrifying) truth about the peaks and pitfalls your website is capable of delivering for your company, and the subsequent impact on your online success.

I've included exercises for you to follow and questions to ask in your pursuit of an outstanding website which represents you perfectly (and authentically) online, digging deep into the "why" or mission which inspires you to get up and run your business every day. And I celebrate you for that - it can be challenging, sometimes lonely, but it is always worth it so never stop learning in this way.

Go back and revisit any exercises you skipped, grab a journal and work through them in one place so you can go back and review at a later date if need be, but do the work. It will pay off.

It's been my pleasure to share some of the incredible stories I've encountered from my most valued clients, who were generous enough to trust me and my team with their time and money to make their vision a digital reality. I believe we learn as much from those who fall down as those who climb up so I'm grateful to have been able to share here the winning strategies for online success as well as the pitfalls to avoid along the way, may they act as markers along the roadside for you as you travel on.

We've shared how great it can be when you get it right, plus how to pause and reboot when things don't go so well. This is the beauty of the internet of course, whatever you publish may indeed be "out there forever more" but you can always go back and edit, refine and course-correct before moving ever forward. This is just one of the aspects of my industry I really love; every day can be a do-over, every night is New Year's Eve!

WHAT WILL YOU DO TOMORROW?

NEXT STEPS AND FREE RESOURCES

I STARTED MY COMPANY TO GIVE EVERY BUSINESS ACCESS TO THE LEVEL PLAYING FIELD OF THE INTERNET

I just loved how a one-man-band could look as big as an orchestra online, BUT that doesn't mean you need to know how to play every instrument!

You may be one of those rare business owners I meet who say "I LOVE technology!" ...and you're happy to dive into what I've shared here in this book, starting today. Or maybe you ARE technically-minded, but don't genuinely have the time to put all of this into practice? Even if you did - is this *really* the best use of your time?

THE POINT IS, EVERYONE IS DIFFERENT

Although you now know the essential ingredients for a successful website, putting them all into practice may not be your idea of fun. That's where we come in.

My team and I create award-winning, expectation-beating websites for companies just like yours every day - could we be the outsourced in-house web team you've been looking for?

PERHAPS SO

...but you're still wondering if you could do this yourself?

...I mean, you have all the ingredients you need now, right?

...and what about that guy in the local paper, couldn't he do it?

LET'S MAKE THIS EASY FOR YOU:

I believe your time is valuable. I believe the best use of your time is putting your experience and love for what you do where it matters most and serves the greatest number of people - into your business. Your input, viewpoint and knowledge are unique to you, no-one else can deliver that - everything else in your business (and this was a hard lesson I had to learn personally), can and *should* be delivered by someone else. Are you ready to let us help you with this?

Start by visiting www.websitemasterybook.com where I have put a whole host of useful resources and bonus content for you, including:

- A secret unpublished chapter to help you find the right help for your business right now
- Access to my previously-published ebook on how to Leverage Your Expertise Online to create new income streams through your website, using what you *already know*
- Find out if you're ready to make this next big leap in your business by taking our free online strategy assessment - a short set of questions designed around the five key stages of a successful website described in this book. This gives you a customised report and access to training videos to help speed up your progress
- Book a discovery call with me and let's identify the next right step for your business on the way to world domination! Too big? How about attracting, connecting and engaging with your ideal clients online? Imagine, no more sifting through the inbox

taking wild stabs at who <u>would</u> be a great client for you or who's really <u>not</u> ready for the uplevelling you offer. Just an inbox filled with pre-qualified, right-fit clients you would love to work with. How would that change your day?

Get to know us. I believe when you love what you do, you're happy to share it with the world, it just comes naturally to me to chew peoples' ears off on any manner of ways to improve their website, increase their enquiries and ramp up those online visitor numbers. I share this freely online in a number of ways:

- check out our YouTube channel at www.youtube.com/@fatpromotions where I regularly post my Website Insight videos to help you supercharge your online efforts - hit Subscribe and Notify to be automatically advised when new content is uploaded that you'll find useful
- sign up to our newsletter at www.websitemasterybook.com to receive bi-monthly free resources by email, including

access to webinars and free downloads to keep you on top of online trends and inspiration

- Reach out to me on LinkedIn at www.linkedin.com/in/fatpromotions-website-design where you'll be the first to see my latest articles about maximising your online presence through smarter strategy - including "burning question" polls and exchanges with other ambitious business owners in my extensive network.

I believe that everything happens for a reason - and there's a reason you're reading this book right now. Perhaps we're meant to achieve great things together? I'm offering a safe, confidential space to discuss whatever challenge your business is facing, and find the way to help you overcome it through a smarter-thinking, harder working website.

Visit www.websitemasterybook.com and let's get out there and show the world what you've got!

ABOUT THE AUTHOR

 Fiona Allman-Treen is an expert in strategic website design and online systems to enable scalable, sustainable growth for business owners and charities globally. Taking the jargon and mystery out of web design is a personal passion, founded on over a decade spent in graphic design and marketing prior to establishing Hastings-based web design agency FAT Promotions Ltd in early 2001.

The Company designs and creates bespoke websites and online software systems to elevate small – but ambitious - business owners to the next level, with a hard-working website to take work off their desk and attract quality clients, enquiries and sales every day. Fiona can often be heard to say a website has to "earn its keep" - a throwback expression from her early years in the North-East of England, meaning (roughly) it has to serve a purpose and generate a good return on investment.

In over two decades, the Company has delivered countless online solutions to private companies, exceeding sales goals and expectations through her strategic approach and endless ability to generate new ideas to remove the "work" and simply do more business.

The Company has a growing speciality in working with charities and non-profits, combining an appealing public-facing web presence with clear calls to action or engagement, as well as online bespoke software systems to help manage volunteers, trustees, staff or multiple locations.

One achievement Fiona is most proud of was convincing a UK government department to evolve their initial plan to deliver in-person training to communities into a custom-made online learning system, immediately prior to the 2020 global pandemic. Without this system, the project could not have met its directive due to UK public movement restrictions, leaving communities vulnerable without this vital scam-prevention and protection training. Instead, the online solution delivered training to **over one million** members of the public, protecting countless others and exceeding all targets.

In every site worked on, Fiona will tell you that she lives vicariously through *their* success, not her own.

An established presenter and devout believer in encouraging ambition and entrepreneurship in young people, Fiona is a sought-after speaker in schools and further education, as well as offering real-world work experience placements to students considering a career in technology. She is also the author of the eBook Leverage Your Expertise Online and creator of the online course to accompany this.

In 2019, Fiona founded the Affinity Business Initiative to support fellow businesswomen in her local area, bringing together women business owners to share, solve, and inspire through their experience. This safe, confidential space to mastermind together on challenges around the core pillars of running a business, gave every individual female business leader a virtual board of directors to problem-solve with and led to lasting friendships and changed lives. The groups still meet today – see www.affinitybusinessinitiative.co.uk.

Formerly a volunteer Business Mentor for The Prince's Trust and The Fredericks Foundation, nowadays in her spare time Fiona is a volunteer dog walker for The Cinnamon Trust (helping the elderly and terminally ill to care for their pets – read more about their great work at www.cinnamon.org.uk) - loves classic cars, red wine and plays the ukulele. If you find yourself in Hastings on a Friday night, twice a month you will find her running the Hastings Old Town Ukulele Group, a free community music group for all abilities aged 18 to 108 – come and sing along!

Proud mum to one incredible daughter, Fiona lives in Hastings, East Sussex, UK, with her (endlessly patient) husband, plus multiple cats, dogs, tropical fish and Horatio the tortoise.

CONNECT WITH ME

Website: www.fatpromotions.co.uk

Email: info@fatpromotions.co.uk

Facebook: www.facebook.com/fatpromotions

Twitter: twitter.com/fatpromotions

LinkedIn:
www.linkedin.com/in/fatpromotions-website-design

Instagram: www.instagram.com/fatpromotions

YouTube: www.youtube.com/@fatpromotions